THE RING CYCLE TAROT

Created by
ALLEGRA PRINTZ

Based on Archetypes from
RICHARD WAGNER'S
Four-Part Music Drama
The Ring of the Nibelung

Cards Adapted from
Wagner's Ring Illustrations of
ARTHUR RACKHAM

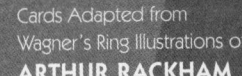

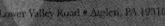

Copyright © 2015 by Allegra Printz
Library of Congress Control Number: 2015930394

All rights reserved. No part of this work may be reproduced or used in any form or by any means—graphic, electronic, or mechanical, including photocopying or information storage and retrieval systems—without written permission from the publisher.

The scanning, uploading, and distribution of this book or any part thereof via the Internet or via any other means without the permission of the publisher is illegal and punishable by law. Please purchase only authorized editions and do not participate in or encourage the electronic piracy of copyrighted materials.
"Schiffer," "Schiffer Publishing, Ltd. & Design," and the "Design of pen and inkwell" are registered trademarks of Schiffer Publishing, Ltd.

Designed by Danielle D. Farmer
Type set in ArnoldBoeD/Chopin Script/Gill Sans

ISBN: 978-0-7643-4817-4
Printed in China

Published by Schiffer Publishing, Ltd.
4880 Lower Valley Road
Atglen, PA 19310
Phone: (610) 593-1777; Fax: (610) 593-2002
E-mail: Info@schifferbooks.com

For our complete selection of fine books on this and related subjects, please visit our website at www.schifferbooks.com. You may also write for a free catalog.

This book may be purchased from the publisher. Please try your bookstore first.

We are always looking for people to write books on new and related subjects. If you have an idea for a book, please contact us at proposals@schifferbooks.com.

Schiffer Publishing's titles are available at special discounts for bulk purchases for sales promotions or premiums. Special editions, including personalized covers, corporate imprints, and excerpts can be created in large quantities for special needs. For more information, contact the publisher.

Card images used with kind permission from Dover Publications from Rackham's Color Illustrations for Wagner's "Ring" (1979)

The Ring Cycle Tarot
Is Dedicated with Gratitude to Ludwig II of Bavaria...

...the so-called "mad" King, whose patronage financed Wagner's completion and initial production of the monumental *Ring Of The Nibelung*. In supporting art over war, Ludwig II left all of us a profound and enduring legacy of music and myth.

Acknowledgments

This deck is published with grateful thanks and much appreciation to:

My brother, John Glenn Printz (1941–2013),
who introduced me to great classical music and Wagner's *Ring Cycle*

~ and ~

SF BATS (San Francisco Bay Area Tarot Symposium):
Thalassa, Mary Greer, Rachel Pollack, Jim Wanless

All The DAUGHTERS of DIVINATION,
especially Rae Martin and Will Heyser

More Thanks To:

Dick Cooke and Claire-Marie Levine of Sunrise Books, Berkeley, California
Ageless Wisdom Study Group: Ford Boyer, Kent Hammerstrand, David Kesten, Frances Harriman and Max
The Sunday Tarot Group: Tim Corfey, Barb Disco Chacon, George and Amalia Vassiliades, and Tess Daniel
Other Supporters: Ian Jackson, Annabella DeMattei, Stephanie Keys, Julianne Maurseth, Ariel Spilsbury, Marilyn Weeks,
and especially Dinah Roseberry for her unwavering editorial support over a period of years.
My Open Secret Bookstore Compatriots: Joelle, Carmen, CeCe, and Sarah

And Priceless Tech Support From:

Nikki Wolfe, Susan Austin, Barb and Diego Chacon, Dana Cilmi, my former neighbor Karl, and the San Rafael, California
Public Library Staff

Prophecy of Voluspa, The Seeress

"Hear me, all ye hallowed beings,
Both high and low,
THE FATES I FATHOM,
YET FARTHER I SEE."

—*Icelandic Poetic Edda 9th–11th Cent. C.E.*

Contents

Preface and Introduction 8

PART I: THE EPIC BACKGROUND 11

1. On My Card Choices 12
2. Circle of Ring Possession: Through the Epic 13
3. Laying Out the Cards 15
4. Plot Synopses of the Four-Part *Ring of the Nibelung* 16

   Prologue: The Rhinegold 16
   The Valkyrie 22
   Siegfried 33
   Twilight of the Gods 45

PART II: THE CARDS & Divinatory Meanings 65

1. Divinatory Meanings of the 78 Cards 67

2. Ring Cycle Tarot Spreads 196

   The 3 Norns Spread 196
   The Nibelung Smithing Spread 198
   Ring Magical Implements Spread 200

PART III: APPENDICES 202

1. Quick Reference Card Meanings 203
2. Biography of Arthur Rackham (1867–1939),
   Ring Illustrator 225
3. *The Ring's* Great Themes 228
4. Wagner's *Ring* Music 240
5. Musical Listening Suggestions 248
6. Bibliography 250
7. Epilogue 254

Preface and Introduction

I.

I saw my first (televised) *Ring* production as a teenager and, from the first moment, I was immediately swept up in its vast mythic scale and exalted music. While I had no clue as to who those Nordic gods, heroines, and heroes were, or the detailed plot line, it didn't really matter. I knew I was witnessing a profound and deeply beautiful artistic masterpiece. Veils dropped, as whole new mythic and sonic worlds opened up before me…

A decade later, passing the display window in The Provincetown Bookshop, I spied the newly published Dover paperback of Arthur Rackham's Ring Illustrations. Entirely captivated, I immediately rushed in and purchased it without a second thought. It has remained a treasure through many moves over the intervening years.

In 1990 I viewed the San Francisco PBS television broadcast of The Metropolitan Opera's superb *Otto Schenk Ring Cycle* production, which rekindled my earlier enthusiasm and interest in this intricate saga. So, several years later, in an effort to deepen my knowledge of *The Ring*, I enrolled in a JFK University extension course, "Wagner's Ring and European Buddhism."

In the meantime, I had become passionate about Tarot and experienced using it.

A paper was required for this course, but as I entirely lacked any enthusiasm for writing whatsoever at that moment, I began idly leafing through my old Dover paperback of Rackham's 1911–12 Ring Illustrations, acquired many years previously, for some inspiration…

AND THEN I SAW THEM:
THE TAROT TRUMPS!

I witnessed a magical parade of the Tarot Major Arcana archetypes, as they leapt out at me from the page: there was Siegfried, the innocent FOOL; Loge the cunning MAGUS; Erda the ancient HIGH PRIESTESS; Wotan the worldly EMPEROR and his consort, the EMPRESS Fricka. They were all announcing themselves to me, and it all made perfect sense! Why not a Wagner's *Ring Cycle Tarot*?

I, for one, would buy it in an instant! After all, there are all sorts of far-flung Tarots exemplifying everyone's favorite interest or obsession—that included baseball, cats, dragons, Alice in Wonderland, The Arthurian legends, William Blake, Halloween, Silicon Valley, Rock and Roll, and vampires, to name but a few.

Surely a *Ring Cycle Tarot* was an empty niche that needed filling?

Besides, a Ring Tarot would have the added unique feature of a dedicated accompanying renowned orchestral and operatic score!

Instead of writing that paper, I immediately set to work adapting the initial twelve Ring Cycle Trumps from Rackham's masterful art.

II.

I found that beyond Rackham's extraordinary illustrations, it was the great themes and vast scale in both time and space, the depth of meaning on many levels, and even the hidden esotericism of Wagner's *Ring Cycle* that adapted themselves so well to Tarot. The complete *Ring*, in both text and especially in music, presents a panoramic vision of the soul—exactly what Tarot exhibits when used as a Hermetic tool in the Western Mystery Tradition, or simply in the spirit of "serious play."

Wagner's *Ring* is based on ancient Northern European and Old Germanic myths and medieval texts with timeless primeval, pre-cultural roots. Utilizing these sources, Wagner was able to delve deeply into the human psyche. The Tarot, a wisdom art, is an inventive medium for bypassing the conscious mind, enabling us to gain direct access to the subconscious through the random shuffling and blind selection of the archetypal and elemental cards. The *Ring Cycle's* amazingly contemporary level of psychological acuity and insight (revolutionary for its time, and decades before Freud) makes it an outstanding application for use as a Tarot deck, which is, to quote A.E. Waite, "A book of wisdom disguised as a pack of cards."

Furthermore, *The Ring* speaks to such current experiences as the necessity for the older order (the "ancient fires") of the Piscean Age to recognize and yield to the new incoming qualities of the Aquarian Age in an energetic transition due to precession of the equinoxes. *The Ring*, exemplified by Brunnhilde, counsels a re-balancing of patriarchal regimes with the divine feminine. It explores romantic love and world service. *The Ring* also looks at some timeworn themes that are always with us: racial conflict, the futility of revenge, and the self-defeating struggle for exclusive power, control, and wealth.

Finally, it has come to my attention that Phil Lesh of The Grateful Dead is a *Ring* aficionado, having attended many performances of the entire Cycle. What better testimonial to the relevance of this epic for our time?

III.

But could *The Ring* material be adapted as a useful divinatory tool? This was a question I posed in the early stages of devising this deck. Certainly Rackham's images are riveting, dramatic, and wholly applicable to Tarot, but would they be imbued with the "magic" that diviners associate with it?

As I progressed with the work, however, I saw how deeply an oracular concept is embedded in both Wagner's and Rackham's material. Prophecy and foretelling is one of *The Ring's* great themes—it is what set Wotan off on his quest, during which he fathers the Valkyries, and his subsequent enlightenment about the futility of even godly power. In doing my research, I came across these comments from no less a source than the great German writer Thomas Mann:

Preface and Introduction

[*The Ring*] is a work in which prophecy and divination in the form of Erda and the Norns are central and revered.

[*The Ring*] is a world-poem overgrown with music and soothsaying nature, where the primeval elements (the four Tarot suits of fire, water, air and earth) are the actors.

[*The Ring*] is a work which has proved, on several levels, a prophecy in itself.

("The Sufferings and Greatness of Richard Wagner" from *Essays of Three Decades*)

An interesting synchronicity that occurred to me in the course of this project was that while Rackham knew nothing about Tarot, he produced his *Ring Illustrations* in the years overlapping Pamela Coleman Smith's work on her famous art for the "Rider-Waite" Tarot. While the two did not know each other, nor did Rackham have any knowledge of Tarot, I cannot help but think that the British metaphysical *zeitgeist* of those Golden Dawn-inspired years was at work unconsciously, influencing Rackham at his drawing table, so seamlessly is his artistic mesh with Tarot archetypes.

So it is with all this and much more to follow that I make my case for a *Ring Cycle Tarot*. For those already familiar with the complexities of *The Ring*, I hope you will find this deck carefully and knowledgeably thought out and imaginatively constructed. For those encountering *The Ring Cycle* material for the first time, what fun and delight awaits! May this Tarot help you to navigate the intricacies of character and plot in an entertaining and interactive way—and in far less time than it took me! And may *The Ring Cycle Tarot* inspire all who use it to listen to the music, where it all started.

—*Allegra Printz*

PART I
THE EPIC BACKGROUND

1.
On My Card Choices

In crafting a Tarot from the music drama librettos of Wagner and the illustrations of Arthur Rackham, I have made some card choices that are admittedly puzzling at first sight. For those who already know *The Ring*, here I explain my logic—the method behind my apparent madness.

I was limited in my choice of cards by the fact that while Rackham completed sixty-four illustrations, I needed seventy-eight images for a complete Tarot deck. Rackham did not illustrate some characters at all—such as Gunther, the logical choice for the King of Gibichungs; I used his half brother Hagen, the real power and mastermind behind the throne instead.

Rackham illustrated others such as Fricka only once; while he depicted Brunnhilde and Siegfried many times at different stages of this multi-generational epic. Since I used the single illustration of Fricka for the trump III Empress, I decided on Brunnhilde, as Wotan's "true will" and favorite daughter for the Queen of Gods—my suit of fire. No one else in my estimation but Brunnhilde could qualify as the Fire Queen.

So, it is necessary to understand that this deck is a creative interpretation and manipulation of the images, using the material at hand. It is not meant as a neat one to one correspondence to *The Ring Cycle*, but is instead a creative and imaginative work of its own, utilizing the depth and genius of both Wagner and Rackham.

Because of the limited number of illustrations, I was forced to employ some playful artistic license in crafting this Tarot. I manipulated some of Rackham's illustrations by cutting them in half to produce two cards, cropping others, collaging, and adding hand-painting for color enhancement. For cards with characters that don't exactly match the race of their suit, my strategy has been to describe their connection with that race/suit, either through the story line or the traditional card meaning for that suit.

Certainly other card choices than those I have made are entirely possible (such as Brunnhilde and Siegfried for the Lovers of trump VI, rather than my choice of the twins Sieglinde and Siegmund), but these are the ones on which I have settled after much consideration.

My goal has been to devise a useful, informative and transformative divinatory tool from this rich material, while remaining completely true to the spirit of both Wagner and Rackham. I have made my card choices thoughtfully, so please stay with me, as all will be revealed…

2.
CIRCLE OF RING POSSESSION Through the Epic

Rhinemaidens are charged with guarding the precious Rhinegold.

Alberich steals the Rhinegold from the Rhinemaidens by foreswearing all love forever. He then forges the gold into the fateful Ring of Power.

Wotan, by employing Loge's wile and trickery, forces The Ring from Alberich, who places a murderous curse on it. But at Erda's bidding, he reluctantly gives it up to the giants Fasolt and Fafner as part of their payment for building Valhalla.

Fasolt immediately seizes the Ring for himself from the treasure pile of Valhalla payment.

Fafner, angry, jealous, and greedy, immediately kills Fasolt for the Ring, initiating Alberich's deadly curse!

Siegfried after an intervening period of nearly twenty years, obtains the Ring by slaying Fafner, who had used the Tarnhelm to turn himself into a dragon, the better to guard his treasure hoard.

Brunnhilde receives the Ring as a love token from Siegfried, who has no real comprehension of its origin, history, or power.

Siegfried, having drunk the Potion of Forgetting and wearing the Tarnhelm, now appears in the guise of Gunthur, and forces The Ring from Brunnhilde.

Brunnhilde reclaims The Ring from the hand of the murdered Siegfried as he lay on his funeral pyre. Wearing it, she then makes a sacrificial leap mounted on Grane into the consuming fire.

Rhinemaidens retrieve The Ring from the mighty Rhine surge over-flowing its banks and cleansing all Nature, after the purifying funereal fire has destroyed the Gods and their world.

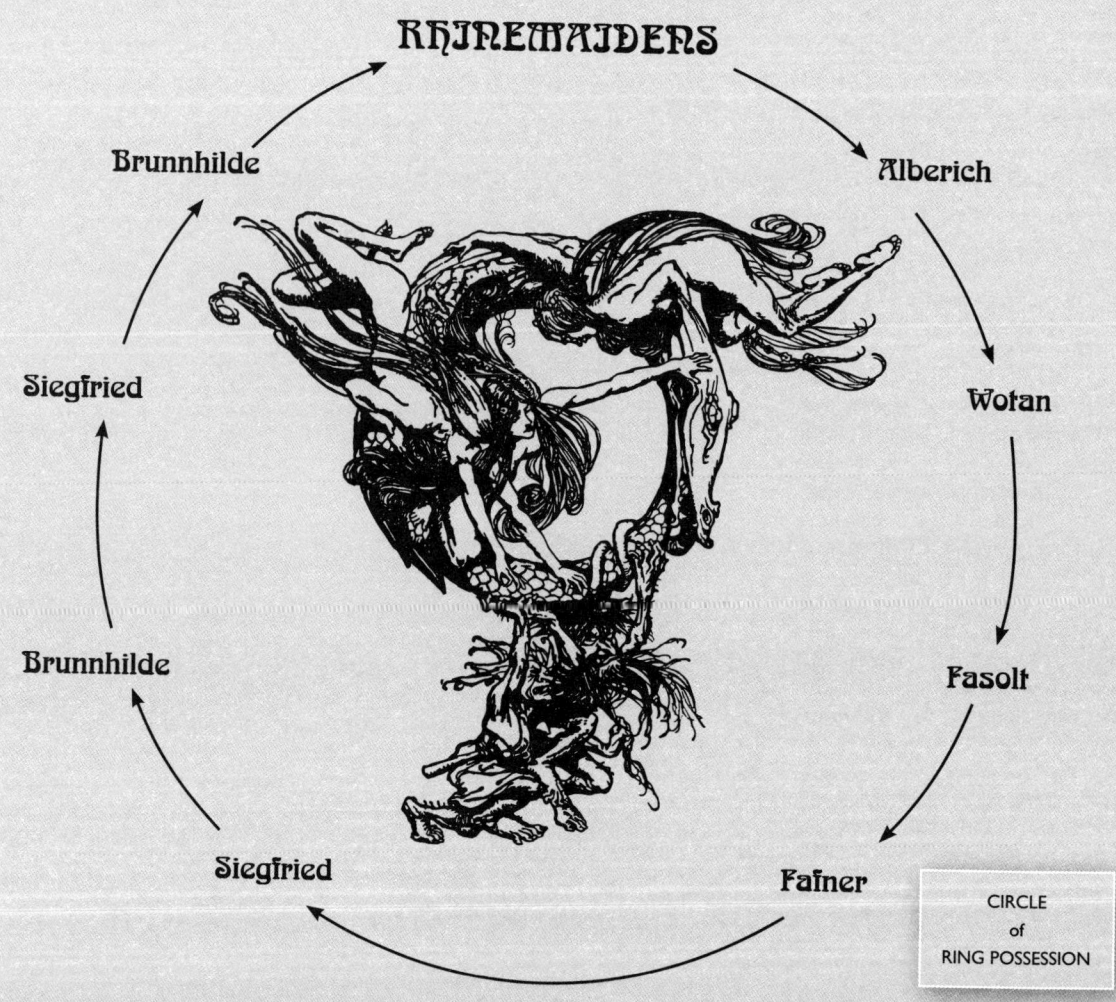

3.
Laying Out the Cards

(A Strategy for Understanding this Deck in Relation to Wagner's Ring *Libretto)*

To Begin Using This Deck

Since the story line of Wagner's *Ring* tetrad is a complicated epic covering several generations, and not widely known in the U.S., I have attempted to walk the reader through it by inserting the relevant *Ring Cycle Tarot* cards as they occur in the unfolding narrative.

In this way you can lay out the entire deck as you read, gaining a better understanding of just how the illustrated cards relate to the entire cycle. Some trumps (noted with an asterisk) are inserted in more than one music drama because they recur in the storyline.

The use and interpretation of this Tarot is greatly enhanced by a familiarity with the characters and events of Wagner's libretto. Back-story knowledge of the cards can stimulate and suggest new insights and revelations in readings. The more deeply you engage the myth, the greater the divinatory resonance of this deck will be.

Especially for those with no prior knowledge of Wagner's *Ring Cycle*, I recommend initially taking the time to lay out the cards according to the following synopses. In addition to providing a timeline, this process will eliminate much initial confusion about the characters in the cards and significantly illuminate their meanings in divination.

I offer a shortcut, however, for those eager to cut as soon as possible to the divinatory chase! Choose a spread (your own or one in this book), shuffle the deck, lay out your cards, and access the Quick Reference Card Guide at the beginning of the Appendices for their core meanings. But keep a record of your cards, so you can fill in as much story and character detail as you like later on for a fuller reading.

HAVE FUN!
AND MAY FATE AND FORTUNE SMILE ON YOU!

4.
Plot Synopsis of the Four-Part Ring of the Nibelung

Prologue: *The Rhinegold*

RELEVANT TAROT CARDS:

Trumps/Major Arcana
- I MAGUS—LOGE
- II HIGH PRIESTESS—ERDA
- III EMPRESS—FRICKA
- IV EMPEROR—WOTAN
- XIV MAGIC—TARNHELM
- XV DEVIL—RING of POWER
- XVII STAR—FREIA
- XVIII MOON—RHINEMAIDENS
- XIX SUN—NATURAL RHINEGOLD

Court Cards
- SUIT of GODS (wands)
  - KING Wotan
  - KNIGHT Loge
  - PAGE Thor
- SUIT of NIBELUNGS (disks/coins)
  - KING Alberich

Pips/Minor Arcana
- SUIT of GODS: Ace, 4, 5, 7, 9, 10
- SUIT of GIBICHUNGS (Swords): 4, 5, 7
- SUIT of NIBELUNGS: Ace, 2, 3, 4, 10

PROLOGUE:
The Rhinegold

SCENE 1—
THE GOLD IS STOLEN

*I*n the beginning was the Rhine, followed soon after by Wagner's long sustained E-flat note and arpeggio. Alberich, a miserable dwarf, scrambles along the ancient riverbanks, and spies the three Rhinemaidens cavorting in the pristine pre-industrial Rhine waters (4 of GODS). They are sublime and graceful creatures, more water sprites than mermaids, by name Vellgunda, Voglinda, and Flosshilde. Alberich, a subterranean creature of the deep earth, is immediately fascinated with them and attracted to their beauty.

One of the Rhinemaidens sees Alberich and calls out to him. A feigned flirtatious dialog ensues (4 of GIBICHUNGS), which the maidens see as a harmless prank, but which Alberich experiences as a cruel humiliation. Each of the three Rhinemaidens in turn pretends romantic interest in the dwarf, who takes their enticements seriously. One by one they bait him, then swim just out of his lustful reach, ridiculing and laughing at him (5 of GIBICHUNGS).

Just at that moment a beam of sunlight strikes and illuminates the subaqueous Rhinegold, which the Rhinemaidens are charged with guarding (XIX SUN—NATURAL RHINEGOLD). Immediately, Alberich's attention shifts to the glittering gold, and he begins inquiring about it. Believing they are in a position of strength and invulnerability, the Rhinemaidens unthinkingly reveal the secrets of the Rhinegold: from this gold one could forge a Ring of Power (XV DEVIL— RING of POWER) conferring on its wearer absolute world power and unlimited wealth. Alberich is all ears. But, they continue, such a ring could never be made, except by one who forswears all love forever. Now, the Rhinemaidens ask, who could possibly do that?

Seriously miscalculating, they continue mocking Alberich, perceiving him as a harmless, gullible fool.

But suddenly, fueled by deep hate and revenge, Alberich dives into the river, renouncing all love forever as he seizes the Rhinegold and makes off with it. The Rhinemaidens, who were off their guard, are rendered frozen in shock by his brazen act. A belated pursuit fails (4 of NIBELUNGS).

Without the gold, the Rhine goes dark. We hear the Rhinemaidens screaming in consternation over the loss of their treasure.

SCENE 2—
PAYMENT FOR VALHALLA COMES DUE

*W*otan, King of the gods (IV EMPEROR) and his consort, Fricka (III EMPRESS), awaken in the morning dawn to see the lofty spires of their newly built castle, Valhalla, shining upon the mountain heights

4.
Plot Synopsis
of the Four-Part Ring of the Nibelung

(ACE of GODS). Ever the realist, Fricka asks Wotan how he plans to pay for it? Wotan admits to cutting a secret deal in which he has promised the builder giants Fafner and Fasolt the goddess of beauty Freia as payment for constructing Valhalla.

Fricka is aghast! Besides the fact that Freia knows nothing about the deal—and has never agreed to it—there's an even more ominous sticking point: Freia alone can tend the Apples of Immortality keeping the gods young and alive (XVII STAR—FREIA). Without her, the gods will soon grow old, sicken, and die. Not to worry, Wotan assures Fricka. He's engaged the trickster fire elemental, Loge (I MAGUS—LOGE) to find a cunning way out of the contract. But Loge is nowhere to be seen, and the giants approach demanding their payment.

After an awkward interlude, Loge makes a belated appearance, but it's evident that he hasn't yet formulated a way out of the agreement. Wotan berates him for his failure; Loge however recounts how on his travels to the far ends of the earth to find a substitute payment equal to the goddess Freia, he did hear of a golden Ring forged by the dwarf Alberich that confers world power and unlimited wealth. Seeking restitution of their gold, the Rhinemaidens had earlier implored Loge (Knight of Gods) for help, naively overestimating his interest in world justice.

The idea of such a Ring of Power secretly inflames Wotan's imagination with an obsessive desire for it. Openly, however, he talks only of the great Nibelung treasure hoard. Overhearing all this, the giants are intrigued with such a fortune; perhaps they would accept this treasure in exchange for Freia—but only after seeing it.

Wotan is really in a bind. Since the Nibelung hoard belongs to Alberich, as a substitute for Freia it's off the table. Loge, however, calmly suggests that he and Wotan simply steal it! After all, Loge glibly rationalizes, Alberich stole the means of that fortune from the Rhinemaidens in the first place, so the hoard is not technically his. Wotan, desperate to keep Freia from the giants, buys into this sophistry. He and Loge agree that once they have secured the wealth, they will then restore the Ring to the Rhinemaidens. Already, however, Wotan has no real intention of doing so, but he conveniently glosses over that part of Loge's plan.

The giants meanwhile grow impatient. They grab Freia by the wrist and announce as they stride off with her, that she will remain in their possession until Wotan can ransom her (7 of GODS). As the gods immediately begin to age (5 of GODS), Wotan and Loge set off hurriedly for the Nibelung realm by way of a deep cleft in the earth (ACE of NIBELUNGS).

PROLOGUE:
The Rhinegold

SCENE 3—
DIRTY TRICKS SECURE A RANSOM

Deep underground, Loge and Wotan discover that Alberich has become a brutal tyrant, enslaving his fellow dwarves into endlessly mining and fashioning gold artifacts for him (KING of NIBELUNGS—ALBERICH). He has even enslaved his own brother Mime (2 of NIBELUNGS). The Ring has magnified his worst character flaws.

The two gods encounter the hapless dwarf Mime (3 of NIBELUNGS), who has just finished crafting a magical helmet, the Tarnhelm, made to Alberich's specifications. One of three supernatural powers it conveys is invisibility. The others are shape-shifting and instant transport.

Mime had hoped to use it himself to usurp Alberich, but could not act quickly enough. Alberich is delighted with the helmet, using it to spy on his workers without being seen (XIV MAGIC/ART—TARNHELM).

When he spots Wotan and Loge, Alberich is immediately suspicious. Wotan tries to reassure him that they'd heard of Alberich's fabulous wealth and wanted to see if it really existed.

Alberich promptly informs Wotan that he plans to use it to gain control of the entire planet and then defeat the gods. "Beware the armies of the night, when the Nibelung hoard shall rise," he threatens. While Alberich's dark ambition stuns Wotan, Loge is scheming away. What, he asks Alberich, is to prevent someone from stealing the Ring while he sleeps? Alberich boasts that this is easily handled, since the Tarnhelm also allows him to assume any shape at will. Loge pretends to doubt such a possibility and asks for a demonstration. Alberich, only too happy to display his superiority before these troublesome gods, dons the helmet, and in seconds transforms himself into a huge writhing serpent (KING of GODS—WOTAN). Feeding Alberich's ego, Loge pretends to be terrified, and pleads for his life (9 of GODS). Alberich then returns to his true form overly pleased with himself.

"Impressive!" affirms Loge, but he can't help wondering if Alberich could also turn himself into something small, like a toad? "No," he continues baiting the dwarf, "Probably too difficult."

Alberich, of course, rises to the challenge by changing himself into a tiny toad. Whereupon Wotan quickly traps him beneath his foot. Loge then quickly binds him, and removing the Tarnhelm, the two conspirators drag the imprisoned Alberich up to the surface world.

4.
Plot Synopsis
of the Four-Part Ring of the Nibelung

SCENE 4—
THE RING ACQUIRES ALBERICH'S CURSE

*B*ack in their own realm, Wotan and Loge demand the golden Nibelung treasure from Alberich in exchange for his freedom (10 of NIBELUNGS). Alberich reluctantly agrees, thinking to himself that with his magic Ring, he will soon be able to amass another fortune. When his Nibelung vassals have finished transporting all his golden hoard to the surface, Loge demands that Alberich's tarnhelm be added to the pile. Then Wotan demands the Ring of Power from him.

"My life, but not my Ring!" responds Alberich, as Wotan unceremoniously tears it from him and proclaims himself the mightiest of lords! Untied, Alberich's first act of freedom is to add a second curse to the Ring: "Let none rejoice who own the Ring. Let no gleam from it shine on a happy mind!" He adds that, from now on, whoever wears the Ring will be prey to the murderous intent of others bent on claiming its ownership for themselves.

The giants soon return with Freia. While impressed with the piles of golden treasure, but now not fully trusting Wotan, they remain careful. Fasolt and Fafner plant two stakes in the ground centering Freia between them. They demand that the gods fill the designated empty space with enough treasure to entirely hide her from view. Clearly aging with Freia held hostage, Loge and Thor are quick to comply.

When the giants inspect the work, however, Fafner spots a chink in the treasure pile through which he can still see Freia. He demands the Tarnhelm from Loge to cover the gap. The bargain now appears sealed and the gods sigh with relief. But wait!

Fasolt, who had been reluctant to trade Freia for the gold in the first place, says he can still see the gleam of her eye through a tiny gap in the pile (10 of GODS).

Loge protests that they already have all the gold. "Not quite!" says Fafner. "What about the gold ring on Wotan's finger? It will just plug that hole."

Wotan freezes. There is no way he is going to relinquish the Ring of Power to these half-wit giants. Never! From the moment Wotan first heard of the Ring, he was inflamed by an obsessive desire for it. Wotan feels he needs the Ring to maintain and fortify his power and authority over the world, and he steadfastly refuses to give it up.

Not knowing the true nature of the Ring, the other gods, sickening and aging, are aghast at Wotan's refusal to complete the ransom of Freia. They implore their King to listen to reason. But Wotan is unmoved.

Prologue:
The Rhinegold

Just as the giants prepare to leave with Freia in hand, an eerie blue light suddenly suffuses the entire area. Erda, a mysterious ancient oracle from the depths of the earth, arises from a fissure that has opened in the ground (II HIGH PRIESTESS—ERDA). She urgently addresses Wotan: he must yield the Ring! It is cursed and will bring only death and destruction to its owner. Everyone listening, including Wotan, is stunned. But he at least has the presence of mind to ask Erda how she knows all this.

Erda declares that her lore is deep and great. She knows the past, present, and future as a timeless Vala (an ancient female prophetic spirit). The dire times have directed her to warn Wotan of the imminent doom of both the gods and his realm. Again she urges Wotan, "Give up the Ring!" And with that, she begins sinking back into the earth. Wotan, however, is unsatisfied; he tells Erda he wants to hear more. Erda replies that Wotan has heard well enough—he must take her warning seriously. Then she vanishes down the fissure.

Wotan attempts to follow Erda, but Fricka and Froh restrain him. When they ask him what he thinks he is doing, Wotan replies that he wants to know all things. Fricka thinks this is utter madness. Thor advises Wotan to listen to the wondrous Erda and forfeit the Ring. Wotan thinks for a bit and, to the relief of all the gods, finally throws the Ring onto the ransom pile almost as an afterthought. The giants release Freia and the gods welcome her back with rejoicing.

But Fasolt and Fafner immediately begin arguing over the Ring. Wearing it, Fasolt claims ownership because he bought it with Freia's glance. In response, Fafner raises his club (7 of GIBICHUNGS), striking his brother with it and killing him. The onlooking gods are horrified. The cursed Ring has already claimed a victim! Without any apparent remorse, Fafner greedily begins scooping up the treasure into a large carrying bag.

To distract the gods from the homicide, Thor throws his hammer to summon a thunderstorm. (PAGE of GODS—THOR) When it clears, a rainbow bridge appears spanning the mountain heights, providing the gods access to Valhalla.

In a celebratory mood, Wotan leads the party of gods across to the new palace. But Loge hangs back, observing them cynically, noting that the gods hasten only to their doom.

The Rhinegold ends, as it began: with the Rhinemaidens. Beneath the rainbow bridge they attempt to get Wotan's attention by loudly lamenting the loss of the gold that lit their river realm (XVIII MOON—RHINEMAIDENS). Wotan ignores them. And a duplicitous Loge disdainfully informs the Rhinemaidens that, from now on, they must live not by the light of their beloved Rhinegold, but instead only by the light of the gods.

The Rhinemaidens, still bereft of their gold and bitterly disappointed, then amplify Erda's prophecy, darkly declaring the gods to be false and weak, and Valhalla short-lived (XVI TOWER—VALHALLA).

4.
Plot Synopsis
of the Four-Part Ring of the Nibelung

The Valkyrie

RELEVANT TAROT CARDS:

Trumps/Major Arcana
* I MAGUS—LOGE
* III EMPRESS—FRICKA
* IV EMPEROR—WOTAN
V HIEROPHANT—BRUNNHILDE
VI LOVERS—SIEGLINDE & SIEGMUND
VII CHARIOT—GRANE
IX HERMIT—WANDERER WOTAN

XI JUSTICE—WOTAN'S SPEAR
XII HANGED WOMAN—
 BRUNNHILDE BOUND
XIII DEATH—VALKYRIES

Court Cards
Suit of WALSUNGS (cups)—KING Siegmund, QUEEN Sieglinde
Suit of GIBICHUNGS (Swords)—

KNIGHT—Avenging Alberich
Suit of NIBELUNGS (coins)—
 QUEEN Grimhilde

Pips/ Minor Arcana
Suit of GODS (wands)—3, 6, 8
Suit of WALSUNGS (cups)—Ace, 3, 4
Suit of GIBICHUNGS (swords)—9
Suit of NIBELUNGS (coins)—6

Plot Synopsis: The Valkyrie

A generation has now passed since Valhalla was newly built. In this interlude, Wotan has sought out Erda in the depths of the Earth, attempting to understand her dark prophecy. He realizes that with the Ring now loose in the world, the gods are not safe—especially from Alberich's hate-filled revenge (KNIGHT OF GIBICHUNGS—AVENGING ALBERICH).

With Erda, Wotan has now fathered nine fierce warrior Shield Maidens, the Valkyries, who are charged with protecting the gods in Valhalla. To this end, the Valkyries are building their own army of hand-selected human warriors felled in warfare on Earth. They stalk the battlefields for the most courageous recruits. Valkyries can only be seen by combatants about to die heroically in warfare (XIII DEATH—VALKYRIES). These chosen dead human heroes are then transported up to Valhalla on the Valkyries' magical steeds to stand guard for the gods.

Since the end of Rhinegold, Wotan has implemented a strategy to regain the Ring: in addition to the Valkyries, he has also fathered a set of twins, the Walsungs, this time by a human mother. Disguised as a human, Wotan has raised the male twin to be a hero, free from the constraints of law and treaty engraved on his ash spear inhibiting and binding his own actions. Wotan's strategy is that this son, Siegmund, will be able to re-secure the Ring by means he himself is lawfully forbidden to use.

Act I

The Overture begins with an ominous musical theme describing a desperate pursuit.

SCENE 1—

A FATEFUL REUNION

It is a dark and stormy night. A disheveled stranger stumbles through a deep wood into a rough fire-lit hut. Believing it to be deserted—or exhausted beyond caring— he collapses in front of the fire.

Sieglinde enters, surveying the stranger with awe and wonder. She thinks the stranger may be dead, but he calls out for water. While exchanging the cup, their eyes lock and they both experience a puzzling recognition; something deep, but not understood, has been stirred (VI LOVERS—SIEGLINDE AND SIEGMUND).

The stranger explains that he is being hunted, and that he is fleeing only because he lost his weapons in a fight. Telling Sieglinde that her presence is like the sunlight after a dark night, he describes

Plot Synopsis
of the Four-Part Ring of the Nibelung

how bad luck has dogged him all his life. Not wishing to spread his bad luck to Sieglinde, he begins to leave. But Sieglinde assures him that the hut is already the very center of bad luck and persuades him to wait for her husband Hunding. Sieglinde and the stranger marvel at one another, attempting to understand their instant connection.

SCENE 2—
IN THE LION'S DEN

Enter Hunding. Instantly suspicious, he grudgingly extends the stranger the hospitality that is the law of the land. Hunding is unnerved, however, by the uncanny resemblance of this mysterious stranger to his wife. Over dinner, Hunding and Sieglinde ask their guest about his past (3 of WALSUNGS). He relates how he and his father, Wolfe, lived deep in the forest with his mother and twin sister. One day, upon returning from the hunt, they found their home burned to the ground, his mother and sister abducted. Sometime later, in a skirmish with a band of raiders, his father Wolfe disappeared, leaving behind only an empty wolf skin.

Since that time, he has tried to live in several villages, but his personal code was never compatible with that of any community. Alone, he has roamed without friends or family, naming himself Woeful.

The stranger then relates the events that drove him to Hunding's hut. He had responded to a call for help from a young maiden, forced to marry against her will. A fight broke out in which her brothers were killed. The maiden threw herself upon their bodies refusing to leave them. He alone defended her against the angry wedding guests, until he was stripped of his sword and shield. The maiden was subsequently killed, and Woeful fled for his life, managing to elude his pursuers. Then he stumbled upon this hut.

Hunding now proclaims a great irony: he himself was called to the aid of the wedding party to capture the intruding troublemaker Woeful! And while he arrived too late to help, fate has now delivered that very same enemy to his door. Hunding tells the stranger he must now pay for the deaths he caused—they must fight the next morning.

SCENE 3—
THE STRANGER CLAIMS HIS NAME AND HIS SWORD

Without any weapon, the stranger Woeful is now completely trapped. "Where," he rages, "is the sword my father promised me in time of greatest need?" In the midst of his angry fit, however, his eye

Plot Synopsis: The Valkyrie

catches a metallic gleam. He discovers it is the hilt of a sword buried in the tree trunk forming the support for Hunding's hut!

Sieglinde meanwhile steals back into the room and tells Woeful she has given Hunding a sleeping draught (QUEEN of WALSUNGS—SIEGLINDE). Then she relates her own sorrowful tale of how she was carried off as a child by raiders and later sold to Hunding for his wife. But at the forced wedding, a tall stranger in a hat with a patch over one eye, entered the hut uninvited (IX HERMIT—WANDERER WOTAN). Catching Sieglinde's glance, he established a mysterious psychic bond with her. Then he thrust his mighty sword into the trunk of the tree and quickly left. All present tried to dislodge it, but to no avail, and there the sword has stayed for years.

Sieglinde continues saying the sword was meant for a single man, and that man, her savior, stands before her. Woeful will claim it to avenge her shame, misery, and forced servitude. Suddenly, the hut door is blown open by the wind. Woeful and Sieglinde, beckoned by the beauty of the moonlight, step outside.

A rapturous duet ensues in which the twins recognize one another and Sieglinde confers upon the stranger his true name: Siegmund. The two proclaim their deep love for one another. Inspired, Siegmund returns to the hut, and pulls the sword Nothung from the tree (KING of WALSUNGS—SIEGMUND). He tells Sieglinde it is his wedding gift to her. Believing deliverance is at hand, Siegmund and Sieglinde escape into the night. Wagner has created so much sympathy for these two forlorn and ill-treated siblings, that we support them, even in an incestuous love.

Act 2

SCENE 1— FAMILY FEUD

In a wild landscape (ACE of WALSUNGS), Wotan and his favorite daughter, the Valkyrie Brunnhilde, discuss the upcoming battle (5 HIEROPHANT—BRUNNHILDE). Sieglinde and Siegmund are on the run, pursued by Hunding, who will soon find and engage them in a deadly battle. Wotan issues his orders: the Walsungs must win; not only is Hunding to die in the fight, but he is also forever barred from guarding Valhalla in the afterlife. But Brunnhilde catches sight of Wotan's wife, Fricka, fast approaching in her ram-driven chariot (III EMPRESS—FRICKA). "A storm approaches," observes Brunnhilde, as she beats a hasty retreat to hide behind a rock.

"The same old storm," sighs Wotan.

Fricka arrives in a fury. One of her more important godly mandates is to uphold the sacred marriage contract. Hunding has

4.

Plot Synopsis of the Four-Part Ring of the Nibelung

made an appeal to her, citing Sieglinde's betrayal of that contract in adultery and incest.

Fricka has her own personal vendetta here as well, because Sieglinde (along with Brunnhilde and the Valkyries) are Wotan's daughters from his adulteries. Fricka now has an opportunity to punish both her philandering husband and his illicit offspring simultaneously.

Why Wotan does not counter with the argument that Hunding's marriage—being forced upon Sieglinde without her consent—should have no validity, is difficult to understand. Perhaps it partly reflects the mid-nineteenth century cultural mindset when many women were pressured into arranged and forced marriages as a matter of course. At any rate, we see a Wotan, who, while King of the Gods, is all too human. He is trapped in a loveless marriage and attempting desperate schemes to regain the Ring of Power. Here Wotan appears more as a modern beleaguered CEO with his corporation in bankruptcy, than a god king.

Fricka and Wotan continue arguing over Hunding's complaint. Wotan makes the appeal that the twins are guilty only of love. Fricka points out that their love is incestuous and outlawed. Besides, Sieglinde and Siegmund are themselves the result of Wotan's own marriage vow transgressions—how can he put the happiness of these two mere illicit half humans above his full goddess wife and her sacred mandate?

Wotan responds that Fricka is a slave to purely conventional thinking, while he, as King, must creatively ensure the future of the entire Realm. He continues arguing that Siegmund, not bound by the laws and treaties that constrict him, is a free hero necessary to regain possession of the Ring. "Need he remind Fricka that until they possess the Ring, their realm remains in dire peril?"

"Ha!" retorts Fricka, "Siegmund is no free hero—he derives his courage only from you, Wotan. He wields a weapon that you magically empowered, left for him, and then guided him to find. What kind of 'free hero' is that? Without you, Wotan, Siegmund would be nothing but an outlaw. How can you dishonor your own wife and Queen by placing this incestuous love above me?"

Wotan is forced to confront the fallacy of a "free hero" Siegmund. He resignedly asks Fricka what she wants. Fricka demands that Wotan remove his protection from Siegmund and give him up to Hunding. Reluctantly, Wotan agrees to this. In addition, Wotan must agree to prevent Brunnhilde and the Valkyries from aiding Siegmund in any way. When Wotan responds that Brunnhilde makes her own decisions, Fricka says she knows Brunnhilde will obey only Wotan's will. Wotan replies that, in any case, it is now too late to change the outcome of the imminent conflict, because Siegmund has the magic sword he provided and thus he cannot lose. Fricka, however, demands that Wotan remove his magic protection from the sword, so that it will shatter in the upcoming fight.

As a high-spirited Brunnhilde returns, Fricka adds, "And let Brunnhilde protect my honor today and my holy cause! Swear, Wotan!"

Wotan swears the oath and is now pledged to Siegmund's forthcoming death. Satisfied at last, Fricka returns to her chariot,

Plot Synopsis: The Valkyrie

smugly informing the returning Brunnhilde that Wotan now has new orders for her.

SCENE 2—
FATHER AND DAUGHTER HAVE A HEART-TO-HEART TALK

Brunnhilde, returning now to find a changed Wotan—gloomy, sad, and distant—urges him to tell her what is wrong. Wotan laments that even as King of the Gods, he is the least free of all beings, bound by restrictive laws and treaties of his own making. Brunnhilde, never having seen her father in such a dejected mood, begs him to confide in her: "Speak to your own true will," she urges her father (IV EMPEROR—WOTAN).

Declaring that he indeed does speak to himself when he speaks to Brunnhilde, Wotan begins reminiscing about his youth—how he first won the world and then desired love. But here was a great paradox: Wotan discovered that he could not have both power and love.

Wotan next recounts the history of the Ring of Power: how he falsely took it from Alberich to pay for Valhalla. Alberich, consumed with revenge for Wotan, had forsaken all love and now singularly lusts only for the power to dethrone the gods (9 GIBICHUNGS—Alberich).

Wotan continues about how he sought Erda in the earth's depths to learn more about her dire prediction of the gods' coming doom, and there fathered the Valkyries with Erda, whom he had magically subdued. The Valkyries were to assemble an army for Valhalla's protection. In this way Wotan hoped to save his world from destruction. Brunnhilde reminds Wotan that since this security force is now in place, there is no reason to fear.

But Wotan explains that with the Ring stashed in the dragon Fafner's cave (6 of NIBELUNGS), there is no security for their world: even as they speak, Alberich, who forswore all love forever to forge the Ring of Power, schemes to reclaim it. And should that happen, the revengeful and hate-filled Alberich will enslave the gods with his own "armies of the night." So he, Wotan, to prevent this at all costs, begot a free hero to act in his place.

Brunnhilde inquires if Siegmund is that necessary free hero. Wotan responds dejectedly that he originally thought so, but now he sees that Siegmund is nothing more than a projection of himself, for his survival depends upon the magically empowered sword he gave him. Wotan can apparently create nothing that is not himself; his divinity is just an empty glory.

Wotan continues that now he must forsake and betray the son who loves him. And not only that, he's heard a disturbing rumor that Alberich now also has a son by a woman he seduced with gold (QUEEN of NIBELUNGS—GRIMHILDE). Erda predicted that this event would signal the demise of the gods' world. All Wotan has to look forward to is the end…

As his own will is now useless, Wotan commands Brunnhilde to fight only for Hunding and Fricka instead. Unable to accept Wotan's

4.
Plot Synopsis
of the Four-Part Ring of the Nibelung

resignation, however, Brunnhilde reminds Wotan that he loves Siegmund, and has taught her to love him too. It is impossible for her to betray Siegmund.

Uncharacteristically, Wotan suddenly becomes very angry, informing Brunnhilde that she must not defy him. After all, she is his will, nothing more than his instrument, and therefore she must obey. In conclusion, Wotan darkly warns Brunnhilde that his full wrath—which she has never seen—is truly terrible.

With that, he angrily stalks off alone. Brunnhilde suddenly realizes that her armor—which she previously wore so lightly in Wotan's service—now feels very heavy.

SCENE 3—
TWINS ON THE RUN

Deeply troubled by her recently revised orders and Wotan's newfound nihilism, Brunnhilde seeks a high ridge on which to clear her thoughts (3 of GODS). From there she sees the approach of Sieglinde and Siegmund (4 of WALSUNGS).

Sieglinde, on the verge of a complete breakdown, has led Siegmund on a wild chase. Terrified of the pursuing Hunding and now unsure of her own actions, she hears Hunding's hunting dogs relentlessly tracking them. Feeling deep remorse, she pleads with Siegmund to abandon her and leave her to her own fate. She relates a vision of his sword Nothung shattering in the upcoming fight. But Siegmund reassures her that with this sword he will take revenge on Hunding for all he has made Sieglinde suffer. Sieglinde collapses in utter physical and mental exhaustion.

SCENE 4—
BRUNNHILDE DEFIES HER FATHER WOTAN

Brunnhilde now intercepts the fleeing twins, informing Siegmund that soon he will be transported to Valhalla, where he will be reunited with his father to serve heroically beside the Valkyries and all the legendary heroes. Accepting at first, Siegmund then asks if Sieglinde can accompany him. When Brunnhilde says that this is not possible, Siegmund responds that if this is the case, he will refuse to go with Brunnhilde. But Brunnhilde reminds him of the law—once a warrior sees a Valkyrie, his death is certain— Siegmund has no choice.

"Who is to kill me?" Siegmund inquires. When Brunnhilde answers, "Hunding," Siegmund responds that this is impossible, since he has Wotan's magically charged sword Nothung.

Plot Synopsis: The Valkyrie

"Alas!" counters Brunnhilde, "Wotan has removed his magical protection. The God has changed his mind—and now you must die."

Siegmund responds that while he has no fear of death, he has no interest whatsoever in the Valhalla afterlife of "brittle pleasures." He accuses Brunnhilde of heartlessness, and while appearing magnificent, she is only cold and cruel. This cuts Brunnhilde to the quick. When Siegmund tells Brunnhilde there will be no one to protect Sieglinde if he dies, Brunnhilde tries to reassure Siegmund that she herself will look after her. Siegmund, however, cries out that if he cannot kill Hunding with the false sword, he can at least kill Sieglinde and himself with it.

As Siegmund raises Nothung to kill Sieglinde, Brunnhilde blocks his sword with her spear, saving her life. Brunnhilde has never before witnessed such a forceful display of passion, love, and self-sacrifice. She is now won back to Siegmund's and Sieglinde's cause—which truthfully in her heart of hearts she had never wholly abandoned.

Brunnhilde then chooses to defy Wotan's "mere words" and reinstate his original plan, believing Wotan's true will resides in his original mandate to protect the twins. She will save them from Hunding no matter what the consequences! Now assuring Siegmund of luck and victory in the upcoming fight, she rushes off to the place of battle, committed to the survival of the twins.

Ironically, it is not Siegmund but Brunnhilde, here acting from her own inner conviction and in defiance of Wotan's orders, who at this point truly becomes the "free hero" Wotan so desperately desires!

SCENE 5—
THE SWORD NOTHUNG SHATTERS

Sieglinde stirs from her troubled sleep, but still in a twilight state, relives the abduction from her childhood home. In the distance, Hunding calls Siegmund out to fight in Fricka's name. Brunnhilde urges Siegfried on from the sidelines, encouraging him to strike Hunding with a mighty blow from the sword Nothung. But when Siegmund does so, the sword shatters. Hunding immediately kills the unarmed Siegmund. In shock, Brunnhilde sees Wotan lurking just beyond the battleground. Quickly, she gathers up Sieglinde and the two escape on her magical horse Grane (7 CHARIOT—GRANE). Wotan steps forward, cradles his dead son Siegmund for a moment, then strikes Hunding dead with a mere flick of his wrist. He firmly resolves to severely punish Brunnhilde for her disobedience.

Act 3

SYMPHONIC PRELUDE:
The Ride of the Valkyries remains the most popular and recognizable piece of all Wagner's music. It's inspired energy, drama, imagination, and great descriptive power are wrapped inside brilliant orchestration. Here we experience The Valkyries at full gallop (8 of GODS—VALKYRIES).

4.
Plot Synopsis
of the Four-Part Ring of the Nibelung

SCENE 1—
THE VALKYRIES ASSEMBLE

Brunnhilde has defied her father Wotan, King of the gods, and his patriarchal realm, knowing she will have to pay the price. Trying to buy time, however, she rides furiously toward the assigned mountain summit meeting place of the Valkyries. The other eight Valkyries have already assembled there, and wonder what has delayed Brunnhilde. Just as they are about to set off for Valhalla without her, they see her approaching. But instead of a dead warrior, Brunnhilde carries (gasp) a woman! Dismounting, Brunnhilde implores her sisters to help her, as a livid Wotan is in frenzied pursuit. While her Valkyrie sisters think her mad, Brunnhilde hastily commands one of them to act as a lookout: for Wotan, as a great storm, is approaching (XI JUSTICE—WOTAN'S SPEAR).

Again Brunnhilde pleads with her sisters to protect her from Wotan's wrath, relating how she disobeyed his orders to save Sieglinde. Now she asks, which one of her sisters will ride off with Sieglinde to protect her? There are no takers, however, as not one of the other Valkyries would ever consider disobeying Wotan. At this point, Sieglinde regains consciousness, expressing her desire to die. Brunnhilde then informs Sieglinde that she is pregnant with Siegmund's child, who is destined to become a glorious hero. At this news, Sieglinde springs to life begging the other Valkyries to help her. The lookout interjects that Wotan is nearly there.

Since her sisters will not help, Brunnhilde decides her best strategy is to confront Wotan alone, allowing Sieglinde to escape unnoticed on foot into the eastern forest, where the dragon Fafner guards the Nibelung hoard. Wotan avoids the place. Handing her the pieces of Siegmund's shattered sword, Brunnhilde tells Sieglinde that she must endure at all costs for the sake of her unborn son, who will someday reforge it. Thanking Brunnhilde, a reinvigorated Sieglinde hurries away down the mountain.

Wotan arrives in full fury. Brunnhilde's Valkyrie sisters have now at least attempted to hide her in their midst, but Wotan insists that they hand her over. The Valkyries ask Wotan what could Brunnhilde have done that was so terrible? His response is fairly typical of the injured father: his favorite Brunnhilde held an exceptional place among the Valkyries and he, as god King, shared his innermost thoughts and motives with her alone. Now she dares to defy him!

SCENE 2—
WOTAN CRUELLY PUNISHES BRUNNHILDE

At that, Brunnhilde bravely steps forward and submits to Wotan for punishment. Wotan, true to type as the authoritarian father, says

Plot Synopsis:
The Valkyrie

Brunnhilde has only punished herself—by disobeying him. How could she possibly will against him? Here again Wotan exemplifies the parent who cannot disengage from his now-grown child, and who views his progeny as mere extensions of himself.

Stunned that Brunnhilde might have feelings and any will of her own, Wotan asks all too familiarly, "How could any daughter of mine act this way?" In a fit of self-justification, Wotan pronounces his harsh judgment on Brunnhilde: she will no longer be a Valkyrie; she will no longer be a Wish or a Shield Maiden. She is henceforth banished from the Race of Gods. Furthermore, her punishment will begin from that very moment—she is now instantly stripped of her immortality and will become the mere obedient wife of the first man who sees her. At that the other Valkyries shriek in dismay and disbelief, hurriedly riding off lest they suffer the same cruel fate.

SCENE 3—
THE RING of FIRE

Brunnhilde petitions Wotan to soften his punishment. After all, she only carried out his true orders—before Fricka interfered and forced him to change his mind. She knew that Wotan still loved the Walsung and did not want him to die. And it was she, Brunnhilde, not Wotan, who had to face Siegmund and inform him of his doom and Wotan's betrayal. She—not Wotan—directly bore the brunt of Siegmund's distress.

But Wotan is unmoved. He resorts to that old familiar father's guilt-trip of how much responsibility he has born for Brunnhilde's sake, how much companionship and protection he's offered her all her life. How lucky she has been to be Wotan's favorite! Wotan continues on self-pityingly that the joys of the heart are not so easily won—he should know! Brunnhilde has had the freedom to drink of love (thanks to him) while he has drunk only of misfortune.

Brunnhilde defends herself by saying the only order that ever made sense to her was to love what Wotan loved. By exiling her, he will exile half of himself.

"If you are so eager to follow love," retorts Wotan, "then now love the human husband who will claim you."

In an attempt to somewhat soften the blow of her punishment, Brunnhilde petitions Wotan to at least let the man who claims her be in some way worthy of her. But Wotan is steadfast and responds that he will not interfere by choosing her future husband. Brunnhilde then informs Wotan of Sieglinde's pregnancy, hoping to move him and soften his harsh resolve. This ploy fails.

Finally, Brunnhilde asks Wotan to grant her at least one thing: to erect a protective barrier around her, so that whoever claims her must be heroic and fearless. Wotan at first refuses, but, reminiscing

4.
Plot Synopsis
of the Four-Part Ring of the Nibelung

of cherished moments with his daughter, weakens in the end, by summoning Loge to magically manifest a protecting Ring of Fire around Brunnhilde (I MAGUS/MAGICIAN—LOGE).

As Loge kindles the fire and Brunnhilde is put into stasis (XII SACRIFICE—BRUNNHILDE BOUND) Wotan makes two more pronouncements:

"Thus turns a god from his own soul."

"Only he who does not fear my Spear shall ever step through that fire." (6 of GODS—WOTAN)

John Culshaw, a prolific and insightful *Ring* commentator, writes in his CD notes to *The Valkyrie* that love is the main theme. This can indeed be cogently argued, as it does display Wotan's deep love for both Siegmund and Brunnhilde, along with Brunnhilde's deep love for her father Wotan and the Walsung twins, her half-brother and sister.

However, I identify a second theme of *The Valkyrie* that is just as important, as the daughter's rebellion against the father, and against male expectations of feminine subservience and domination by a patriarchy.

Brunnhilde refuses to uphold laws simply for their own sake, or because she is ordered to do so—even by her father the King. Rather than acquiescing to an expedient and self-serving male authority, she does indeed act from her deep love, but also, just as importantly, from the authority of her own truth.

King Wotan's autocratic absolute rule, now riddled with his opportune backtracking and inconsistencies, is crumbling. A new day begins to dawn in the realm of the gods, thanks to Brunnhilde's defiance of misguided male authority.

Siegfried

RELEVANT TAROT CARDS:

Trumps/Major Arcana
- * 0 The Fool-SIEGFRIED
- * II HIGH PRIESTESS—ERDA
- * VII STRENGTH—SWORD NOTHUNG
- * IX HERMIT—WANDERER WOTAN
- * X NORNS—WHEEL of FORTUNE
- * XII HANGED WOMAN—BRUNNHILDE BOUND

Court Cards
SUIT of WALSUNGS (cups) PAGE—Young Siegfried
SUIT of NIBELUNGS (coins)
KNIGHT—Blacksmith Mime
PAGE—Siegfried at Mime's Forge

Pips/Minor Arcana
WALSUNGS—2, 5, 6, 7, 9
GIBICHUNGS (swords)—ACE, 8
NIBELUNGS—5, 6, 7, 8, 9

4.
Plot Synopsis
of the Four-Part Ring of the Nibelung

SCENE 1—
MIME HATCHES A PLOT; SIEGFRIED UNCOVERS HIS PARENTAGE

Another generation has nearly passed. Mime is at work in his forest forge (KNIGHT of NIBELUNGS—MIME) attempting to make yet another sword for his charge, Siegfried, who has now grown to young manhood. But for all Mime's skill the work does not go well and he is frustrated and angry. Siegfried has uncanny strength and shatters every sword he makes. If only he could reforge the broken sword fragments of Nothung that the lost and pregnant Sieglinde, who died giving birth to Siegfried, brought with her years ago when she found refuge in his cave—it would be a sword Siegfried could not shatter. But repairing it has proven impossible. Still Mime begins plotting that Siegfried—armed with Nothung—could slay the dragon Fafner. Then, he, Mime, could claim the Ring of Power and gain revenge, world domination, and the stature he craves.

Suddenly, the brash Siegfried enters the forge, leading a wild bear on a rope as a jest, but striking Mime with terror. Mime points out the newest sword in an effort to placate Siegfried, who quickly releases the bear back into the wild. To Siegfried, the sword proves only a toy and he quickly breaks it. He then launches into a disrespectful diatribe against Mime, who offers him food (9 of NIBELUNGS). When Siegfried swats it away, Mime tries to guilt-trip him, with a reminder of his years of selfless sacrifice for Siegfried his son.

But Siegfried doesn't buy it. A powerful instinct has warned him to distrust Mime's motives. Siegfried has always felt that Mime was evil, and dreaded returning to the forge after playing in the forest among his animal friends. They demonstrate a love and affection for one another that Mime has never displayed to him (6 of WALSUNGS). Furthermore, Siegfried notes, the animal offspring always resemble their parents, but from seeing himself in the reflection of a pond, he knows he doesn't look anything like Mime. (PAGE of WALSUNGS—YOUNG SIEGFRIED) He suspects that Mime is not really his parent, as he has claimed all these years: he demands the truth.

But when Mime is not forthcoming, Siegfried resorts to grabbing him by the throat, forcing the truth from him. So for the first time, Siegfried hears of his tragic mother Sieglinde, whom Mime rescued, (5 of NIBELUNGS) when he found her alone and lost in the winter forest (5 of WALSUNGS—SIEGLINDE); and how she later died giving birth to Siegfried. Mime also tells Siegfried of the broken sword wielded by his dead father, Siegmund. Mime drags out the sword pieces to prove his story. Overjoyed to discover he is not

Plot Synopsis:
Siegfried

related to Mime, Siegfried immediately charges him with the task of reforging Nothung. He then dashes back into the forest. Mime is left to a task, which he knows full well to be impossible for him. Who, he wonders, could possibly accomplish it?

SCENE 2—
MIME LOSES A CONTEST AND FORFEITS HIS HEAD

Wotan, who has been wandering the world incognito and alone since imprisoning Brunnhilde on a fire-ringed rock, now enters Mime's forge. He has been gathering information on both Siegfried the Walsung, and the Ring of Power. In spite of Mime's inhospitable manner, Wanderer Wotan (IX HERMIT—WANDERER WOTAN) suggests a contest of questions and answers. Each will ask the other three questions. He who fails to answer all three correctly forfeits his head to the other. Overconfident and without any thought, Mime asks the Wanderer three questions that are too easy:

What is the name of the race that dwells under the earth? (Dwarves)

What is the name of the race that dwells on the earth? (Giants)

What is the name of the race that dwells above the earth? (Gods)

Naturally, Wanderer Wotan answers correctly, but in so doing he weaves such a detailed history of the Ring of Power that Mime is completely rattled; for the first time, Mime suspects his guest may be much more than he appears.

But now it is Wotan's turn. Mime confidently answers the first two questions:

What race does Wotan love best, but has treated the most harshly? (Walsungs)

What is the name of Siegmund's famous sword? (Nothung)

But he is at a loss for an answer to the third: Who can reforge Nothung? (8 of NIBELUNGS)

...which is, of course, the very question Mime should have asked the stranger but didn't!

The answer is that only *he who knows no fear* can reforge Nothung.

The mysterious stranger has won the contest and Mime, his head now forfeit, is in a complete panic. But Wotan, taking up his spear, departs, saying only that he gives the prize of Mime's head to "the one who knows no fear."

4.
Plot Synopsis
of the Four-Part Ring of the Nibelung

SCENE 3—
SIEGFRIED REFORGES NOTHUNG AND CLAIMS HIS BIRTHRIGHT

Siegfried returns to the forge to check on Mime's progress remaking his father's shattered sword. Of course, Mime riddled with fears, both past and present, now understands just why he is incapable of reforging it. Siegfried is impatient and completely exasperated with Mime. Accusations fly between the two of them. Finally, Mime, remembering the words of the mysterious stranger, asks Siegfried about fear. Has he ever felt anxious, trembling and afraid when alone in the forest? Siegfried replies he has known only joy there, but he is curious as to what the thing is that Mime describes. Could Mime teach him this "fear"? Mime replies it might be possible by means of the dragon Fafner, who lives in a cave not far off (6 of NIBELUNGS).

Enthusiastic at this new opportunity, Siegfried seizes the task of reforging the sword himself. Mime watches with alarm, as Siegfried creates chaos in the forge, commenting that it would have helped if Siegfried had taken the trouble to learn his craft. Undeterred, Siegfried stokes the fire, continuing to work in earnest—with far more impassioned inspiration than any method or technique (PAGE of NIBELUNGS—SIEGFRIED at Mime's Forge).

Mime now grapples with a terrible dilemma. While he needs the services of a fearless hero to slay Fafner for the Ring, the stranger told him that his head is now forfeit to that very hero—his charge Siegfried! How to resolve the situation? Mime's head begins to spin: if the fearless Siegfried reforges the sword and kills the dragon (which Mime thinks is likely), that still leaves Siegfried with the treasure. So how to secure it for himself?

In seconds, Mime hits on a murderous solution: once Siegfried has possession of the Ring of Power, Mime will offer him poisoned refreshment. With Siegfried out of the way, Mime can claim the gold and the Ring!

Meanwhile, Siegfried has succeeded in reforging Nothung and raises it in triumph (0 The Fool—SIEGFRIED)! The astonished and delighted Mime thinks only of how soon—with the Ring—he will be able to claim absolute power as master of the world, exact revenge on his brother Alberich, and finally be compensated for everything that has gone wrong in his life.

Plot Synopsis: Siegfried

Act 2

SCENE 1—
WOTAN AND ALBERICH MEET OUTSIDE FAFNER'S CAVE

A musical prelude plays the low, ominous tones of the dragon motif. Outside Fafner's forest cave, in which the Ring of Power lies unused, the dwarf Alberich keeps a night vigil (8 of GIBICHUNGS). Wanderer Wotan appears amidst a strange light and a rustling of leaves. Alberich tells him in no uncertain terms to get lost. But Wotan makes the astonishing pronouncement that he himself no longer covets the Ring and is now just an impartial observer. Naturally, Alberich does not believe this and wonders what Wotan's real motive is. He informs Wotan he is no longer the same fool that Wotan duped out of the Ring years previously. And he knows that Wotan, restrained by the treaties inscribed on his spear, cannot take the Ring by force. Furthermore, he smells Wotan's fear that he, Alberich, will regain the Ring and enslave the gods with it.

Alberich also reminds Wotan of the curse with which he imbued the Ring: anyone who claims the Ring will die at the hand of another who covets it.

A remarkably relaxed Wotan replies nonchalantly that whoever can claim the Ring is welcome to it! Wary and suspicious, Alberich tells Wotan he knows all about the son he engendered to reclaim the Ring for him.

"It is no longer me you need to fear," responds Wotan, "but your brother Mime. In fact, he is on his way here at this moment with Siegfried—who by the way, will kill Fafner. Siegfried knows nothing of the Ring and is being manipulated by Mime to retrieve it for him. Your brother is your sole rival now."

To demonstrate his good faith, Wotan suggests that Alberich warn Fafner of the approaching Siegfried—in exchange for the Ring. With that, Wotan tries to wake Fafner from a deep sleep. Alberich is astounded at Wotan's actions. But the lure of regaining the Ring trumps all else in his consciousness. He watches as the angry Fafner asks Wotan who dares to disturb him?

Indicating Alberich, Wotan tells Fafner that a friend is here to warn the dragon about a hero who is on his way to slay him. Fafner replies that his empty stomach duly takes note of this.

4.
Plot Synopsis
of the Four-Part Ring of the Nibelung

Alberich now chimes in, saying this hero Siegfried is really only after the Ring. If Fafner will just hand it over to him, Siegfried will then have no motive for an attack. But Fafner, believing himself invulnerable, turns over and goes back to sleep.

Laughing, Wotan tells Alberich he has tried his best, and then offers him some surprising advice: "Fate charts its own course; you can alter nothing." Wotan then disappears into the night.

The hate-filled Alberich, believing himself wiser than Wotan, decides to continue waiting patiently for another chance at the Ring and the day when he will see the demise of that supposedly superior "gang of eternals."

SCENE 2—
SIEGFRIED FIGHTS THE DRAGON FAFNER

Just before dawn of the next day, Mime and Siegfried approach the cave after walking all night. Siegfried is impatient and keeps asking Mime when he will learn the mysterious thing called "fear." Mime tells him that his best opportunity is at hand in Fafner, and he warns Siegfried about the dragon's terrible jaws, its poisonous venom, and strong lashing serpent's tail. Unimpressed, Siegfried wants to know if this dragon has a heart.

"Oh yes," continues Mime, "and a terrible twisted heart it is."

But Siegfried, devising his hunter's strategy, only wants to know its biological location, not its quality. Now completely exasperated with Mime, Siegfried tells him to make himself scarce—in fact forever; Siegfried wants nothing more to do with the dwarf. Mime decides to wait down at the spring where Fafner goes every morning to drink where he can observe the encounter (from a safe distance) between the two.

Relieved to be rid of the irritating Mime, Siegfried surveys the wood with delight. He sinks into a reverie imagining what his real parents might have looked like. Lightly dozing off, he is awakened by the melodious song of a woodbird. Siegfried playfully decides to try to speak to the bird in its own language by fashioning a wooden flute. But the sound he makes is completely off-key, resembling nothing like the beautiful song of the bird. Finally giving up after several more tries, Siegfried decides to use his own hunting horn—something he knows how to play. The horn awakens Fafner, however, and the angry dragon comes crashing out of his cave through the underbrush.

Siegfried asks Fafner if he can possibly teach him fear. In response to such outrageous cheek, Fafner threatens to gobble him up.

Plot Synopsis:
Siegfried

"Then I'd better kill you straight off," declares Siegfried, taking up his sword. The battle begins (7 of WALSUNGS). Fafner spews venom at Siegfried but misses. Then he tries to knock Siegfried over with a swipe of his tail, but Siegfried is too quick, inflicting a painful slicing wound to the dragon's tail instead. When Fafner rears up in shocked response, Siegfried sinks his sword Nothung straight into the dragon's heart.

The dying Fafner asks Siegfried who put him up to this attack, surmising that Siegfried is too young and naive to have plotted it alone. The dragon gives a "'death bed" account of himself and his brother Fasolt, the last of the giants, who will now both be dead in fulfillment of the Curse of the Ring. And Fafner warns Siegfried that he is now in danger of that curse himself.

In his final death throes, Fafner heaves over on his back, allowing Siegfried to retrieve his sword Nothung. But in extracting it from the dragon's heart, Siegfried accidentally spatters himself with dragon blood. Licking it from his hand, Siegfried experiences a taste like "burning fire" (VIII STRENGTH—SWORD NOTHUNG).

A few moments later Siegfried hears the woodbird again—but now he miraculously seems to actually be able to understand what it says! The woodbird instructs Siegfried to go into the dragon's cave and retrieve two items—the Tarnhelm and the Ring of Power. Siegfried returns to the cave to oblige the magical bird.

SCENE 3—
OF DRAGON'S BLOOD AND THE WOODBIRD

While Siegfried searches the cave, Mime steals back into the forest glade and assures himself that Fafner is indeed dead. But watching him is the concealed and ever-vigilant Alberich. So when Mime starts back for the treasure cave, Alberich jumps out, barring his way. The two immediately begin arguing over who owns the Nibelung hoard (7 of NIBELUNGS). Mime claims ownership as recompense for all his years of trouble in raising Siegfried; Alberich retorts it was he who initially stole the Rhinegold and formed it into the Ring of Power.

"Yes, but who crafted the Tarnhelm?" counters Mime.

Mime then proposes that perhaps the two of them could share the treasure: Alberich could have the Ring, if he could have his Tarnhelm. But Alberich, hating his brother, adamantly refuses this offer. The two hide as Siegfried returns with the Tarnhelm hanging off his belt and wearing the Ring on his hand. The woodbird acknowledges Siegfried's recovery of the two important magical items, but he then warns Siegfried to be very wary of Mime. The bird explains how by tasting Fafner's blood, Siegfried has also acquired a new psychic power allowing him to hear Mime's true black thoughts—concealed behind his seemingly harmless words.

4.
Plot Synopsis
of the Four-Part Ring of the Nibelung

The treacherous Mime steps forward and with feigned innocence asking Siegfried if he had learned fear from the dragon.

"No," sighs Siegfried, admitting he's feeling remorse for killing Fafner, while other more wicked villains still live. Mime meanwhile thinks that with Fafner dead, he will now easily poison Siegfried and claim the treasure. Unknown to Mime is that Siegfried can hear the thoughts of his murderous plot.

"You plan to kill me then?" he asks. Surprised, Mime replies that Siegfried has not heard him correctly. He continues thinking how, having always despised the boy, he raised Siegfried solely to use him as the means of regaining the Ring.

"So, I was right in believing you hated me!" asserts Siegfried.

Startled, Mime denies such a thing. Pulling out the prepared poisoned drink and offering it to Siegfried, as he thinks to himself how he will soon have Siegfried's sword Nothung for himself.

"You plan on taking all that I have?" inquires Siegfried.

Now really rattled, Mime scolds Siegfried. Again, he offers the poisoned "refreshment" to Siegfried. But Siegfried, knowing its true purpose, asks Mime how he brewed it.

Mime can't help thinking how his potion will soon put Siegfried into a numbing sleep, in which he can seize the sword, behead the youth, and claim the treasure.

"You'll kill me as I sleep?" asks Siegfried.

"Did I say that?" responds Mime, while clearly thinking, "drink, Siegfried, and die!"

Hearing that, Siegfried draws Nothung, and delivers a killing blow to the murderous Mime. From his hiding place Alberich only laughs mockingly at his brother's death—as yet another of his competitors for the Ring of Power is removed from the playing board.

Siegfried drags the bodies of Mime and Fafner back to the cave and seals the entrance with them. Then, in a break from the morning's arduous encounters, he reclines under a shady tree. He suddenly begins to feel very lonely, thinking how he never even knew his parents—only that treacherous dwarf. Siegfried decides that what he needs now is a loving friend.

He asks the hovering woodbird to help him find a companion.

The woodbird tells Siegfried that he will soon have a caring wife, and describes the sleeping Brunnhilde, surrounded by a ring of fire high atop a mountain. Immediately enchanted, Siegfried asks the bird if he could possibly pass unharmed through the fire and awaken her?

"Only he who knows no fear can achieve it," responds the woodbird.

Plot Synopsis:
Siegfried

Joyfully, Siegfried realizes that exactly describes himself! In a state of excited hope, he tells the woodbird to quickly lead him to the mountain of the sleeping maiden (XII HANGED WOMAN—BRUNNHILDE).

Act 3

The third act of Siegfried in my opinion is pivotal to the entire *Ring Cycle*. Here, Wotan experiences a sudden psychological growth spurt and undergoes a radical character change resulting from encounters with Erda and his grandson Siegfried.

SCENE 1—
WOTAN ASKS ERDA HOW HE CAN CHANGE FATE

In a desolate place at the base of a mountain, a storm rages in the night, exactly mirroring Wotan's disturbed state of mind (ACE of GIBICHUNGS). Wotan has previously sought both power and love, but now he seeks understanding. Anxiously, he magically summons Erda up into the middle world of the gods from her sleep of wisdom in the depths of the earth. Wotan calls upon her as omniscient, eternal, and immemorially wise (II HIGH PRIESTESS—ERDA).

This is a world conception that Wagner took from Old Germanic and Norse literary sources that is very different from the contemporary scientific one. It is the belief that the earth itself is alive and has a transcending consciousness, and that we humans are only small cells within its greater awareness. In antiquity, it was believed that women, with a biology more attuned to the earth, have easier access to that greater knowledge hidden in the chthonic planetary depths, with a time scale vast by human standards. And it is for this level of knowledge that women were revered, acting as guides and oracles to their communities. So Erda with her consciousness rooted deep within the earth, is perceived as all-knowing, all-wise.

(It is not surprising, therefore, that most male *Ring* commentators, including Shaw dismiss the scenes with Erda as superfluous, while I find them riveting and believe they are absolutely integral to Wagner's message. It is the theft of the Rhinegold combined with Erda's prophecy that sets the entire *Ring Cycle* in motion.)

To continue the story line, Wotan tells Erda that ever since she prophesied the god's doom, he has lived in fear of the end of the world. He wants to know how he can master his fear and, more importantly, how he can change her prophecy.

But Erda describes to him how the system works: she acquires her wisdom only by means of her mysterious dreaming, which comprises her entire thought process. From her sleep, dreams, and meditations, Erda finally distills her wisdom. Her daughters, the Norns, in turn, spin the threads of this dreaming wisdom into the

4.
Plot Synopsis
of the Four-Part Ring of the Nibelung

world (X WHEEL of FORTUNE—THE NORNS). The implication is that in spite of being all-knowing, Erda cannot directly control her thoughts, because their source is in the non-rational astral-mystical realm of dreams. Here I identify the feminine pole of consciousness alluded to above—the deep and high intuition from which creativity and divination springs. It does not rely on the male rationality by which Wotan lives and rules, and hard as he tries, he cannot really comprehend Erda's Primal Feminine Numen.

On her side, Erda doesn't answer Wotan's inquiries because she can't honestly process them. In her own world view and system of knowing, Wotan's questions really make no sense. She tells Wotan to go ask the Norns, who at least partially inhabit his own middle world. Wotan points out that the Norns merely spin following her orders and have no power to change anything. Well then, says Erda, ask our daughter Brunnhilde. But Wotan says he can't do that either because he's banished her for disobedience and pride and put her to sleep.

Erda replies that she's a bit confused, since Brunnhilde learned pride and defiance from her father! She asks Wotan how he can possibly justify punishing Brunnhilde for transgressions of which he himself is the shining example?

Now comes the moment in which Wotan experiences his metanoia: in a nearly spiritual conversion he suddenly reverses his position. Wotan may not understand Erda, but he now realizes he can neither control, change, nor evade a power—different and greater than his own—of which she is the direct agent. Wotan recognizes himself for the first time, not as the Supreme Being he thought he was, but instead as a mere demiurge, a secondary power at best. Finding himself squarely in the path of the crushing, rolling wheel of inevitability and unable to change its course, Wotan not only resigns himself to his own demise and that of his realm, but decides his best strategy is to actively embrace it. This is a sea change in *The Ring Cycle*.

Wotan tells Erda that from now on, he wills against his own survival. He relinquishes any further attempt at influencing and controlling the world, and now leaves its fate to Siegfried with the Ring, and to Brunnhilde, soon to become his consort.

In a prophecy of his own, Wotan predicts Brunnhilde will redeem the world with a single act. He then releases Erda from his magic call, allowing her to return to her dreaming deep within the earth unperturbed.

SCENE 2—
Siegfried Shatters Wotan's Spear

Just as Erda disappears, Siegfried approaches following the woodbird in his quest for a companion. Seeing Wotan, he asks him

Plot Synopsis: *Siegfried*

if he knows the way to the rock where a maiden is imprisoned by a ring of fire. Siegfried hasn't a clue as to whom he is speaking, and assumes as Mime first did, that Wotan is a wandering simpleton.

Amused, Wotan decides to give Siegfried a bit of a hard time, inquiring about his recent adventures, while knowing full well all about them. In a series of questions, he tries to help Siegfried comprehend the real source of his reforged sword, Nothung—which is of course, Wotan himself. But the arrogant and impatient Siegfried doesn't quite get it. Showing Wotan no respect, he impatiently orders him out of his way.

But Wotan won't budge, as he's not through with his impetuous grandson just yet. Siegfried again challenges Wotan to move aside. Wotan becomes angered at Siegfried's obtuseness and reveals himself to be the very one who set the fire around Brunnhilde. Then brandishing his spear and further barring his way, he warns Siegfried that his sword Nothung has already been shattered against it once before. Mistaking Wotan for Hunding, the bitter enemy who killed his father, a revengeful and impassioned Siegfried strikes a furious blow at Wotan's spear.

Miraculously, he splits in half Wotan's spear with the world's laws and treaties engraved on it, by which Wotan rules. In the drama of accompanying thunder and lightning, Wotan needs no further confirmation that a new order is about to overtake him. Interpreting his broken spear as an unmistakable omen of the gods' foretold imminent demise, Wotan philosophically collects the pieces of his shattered spear. Meanwhile, a triumphant but ignorant Siegfried races toward the mountain of fire to claim Brunnhilde as his bride.

(The transition between scenes is accompanied by a reprise of the beautiful and exalted "Magic Fire" music.)

SCENE 3—
SIEGFRIED CLAIMS BRUNNHILDE AND LEARNS FEAR

Siegfried quickly pushes through the barrier of fire. When he discovers Brunnhilde asleep on a rock dressed in armor, helmet, and shield, Siegfried naturally mistakes her for a man. In an attempt to make this noble warrior more comfortable, Siegfried cuts away the armor with his sword. But he gasps in wonder when he discovers a woman in feminine dress beneath it. Siegfried takes a stunned step back overcome with a new feeling, realizing it is the long-sought fear!

Now here is a great matter: Who instills fear in the hero Siegfried? Not the wild forest beasts, not the fire-breathing dragon, not even his murderous guardian—BUT A WOMAN, and one who is asleep at that! Wagner may downplay this point, but he has tapped into and laid bare the deep primal fear of the male for the female, that fuels both the historic and current patriarchal psychological

Plot Synopsis
of the Four-Part Ring of the Nibelung

need to dominate, control, restrict, and devalue women. Instead of recognizing the female as a different but equal and integral part of itself, the fear-based patriarchy institutionalizes woman as the lesser—but still exceedingly dangerous—other, whose powers (reproductive and intuitive to name but two) must be controlled.

Wagner, in depicting Siegfried's discovery of Brunnhilde as initially eliciting the emotion fear in him, betrays his own comprehension (on some level) that the irrational fear of the male for the female and its resulting imbalance of energies, is one true source of a deep dilemma in our current civilization, that continually generates dangerous distortion and disharmony. This insight, however, is quickly glossed over.

At any rate, Siegfried now wonders if he is bold enough to wake Brunnhilde and is uncertain just how to go about it. He tries commanding her to wake with his voice but Brunnhilde does not respond. Then he kisses her on the lips and she slowly stirs. Brunnhilde has been sleeping for twenty years, so it takes a while for her to fully awaken.

Here Wagner, in a musical description of Brunnhilde's return to life, wrote some of the most gorgeous and soulful music of *The Ring*.

Brunnhilde, a goodly pagan, makes her first waking act a ritual salutation to the sun. Siegfried announces himself when she next asks who woke her. The two sing a short duet of rapt mutual wonder and recognition. Brunnhilde tells Siegfried she knew his mother and actually protected him even before he was born. So, in a sense she has always loved him. She greets him as a "hero most holy, Light of the World" (9 of WALSUNGS).

But upon seeing her broken armor Brunnhilde becomes extremely distressed, realizing that she has lost all her godly powers and is now completely defenseless. Siegfried tries to reassure her, saying that he himself had no armor when he broke through the Ring of Fire to find her, or when he summoned the courage necessary to wake her. Brunnhilde remains unconvinced. She feels deep anguish, remembering the terrors of her long dark sleep and the loss of her supernatural powers. She asks Siegfried to leave her alone and in peace, as she fears his overwhelming strength will destroy her. But Siegfried, with considerable charm, says it was her wisdom that drew him to her, and describes the life of laughter and joy they could share together.

Brunnhilde is finally won over by Siegfried's ardor, and the fresh new prospect of a personal happiness unconnected with serving the gods. Laughing and now gladly relinquishing her past, including the pomp and circumstance of Valhalla, she wholeheartedly embraces Siegfried as her new destiny. The two pledge to set one another ablaze in mutual love (2 of WALSUNGS).

Yet even amidst all the bright lights and ecstatic high on which the music drama *Siegfried* ends, Brunnhilde sounds an ominous and cryptic note, proclaiming theirs is a love that laughs at death, and a death that is joy—foreshadowing the culminating events of *Twilight of the Gods*.

Twilight of the Gods

RELEVANT TAROT CARDS:

TRUMPS/ MAJOR ARCANA
- * IX HERMIT—WANDERER WOTAN
- * X WHEEL of FORTUNE—THE NORNS
- * XI JUSTICE—WOTAN'S SPEAR
- * XIV MAGIC—TARNHELM
- * XV DEVIL—RING of POWER
- * XVIII MOON—RHINEMAIDENS
- * XX AEON—WORLD ASH TREE
- * XXI—WORLD—THE RING CYCLE

COURT CARDS
SUIT of GODS (Wands): QUEEN BRUNNHILDE
SUIT of WALSUNGS (Cups): KNIGHT—SIEGFRIED AT THE HUNT
SUIT of GIBICHUNGS (Swords): KING HAGEN; QUEEN GUTRUNE PAGE—INNOCENT SIEGFRIED
SUIT of NIBELUNGS (Coins): QUEEN GRIMHILDE

PIPS/MINOR ARCANA
GODS—2
WALSUNGS—8, 10
GIBICHUNGS—2, 3, 6, 10

4.
Plot Synopsis
of the Four-Part Ring of the Nibelung

The last day of the world is near. Just before dawn, the Three Norns are spinning and weaving individual fates and world destiny on a promontory not far from Brunnhilde's rock. (XX AEON—WORLD ASH TREE) As they work passing the strands of past, present, and future to one another, (X WHEEL of FORTUNE—THE NORNS) they begin to converse:

The First Norn laments how once she tethered her cord to the World Ash Tree, watered by a spring. A god came and paid for a drink from its clear waters of wisdom with one of his eyes (IX HERMIT—WANDERER WOTAN). From the World Ash, he then cut off a branch from which to fashion a spear. But alas! His action left an open gash in the tree that did not heal. Eventually, it succumbed to blight and died. Even the spring dried up. Now she must use this poor substitute of a pine tree. What will come of this?

The Second Norn relates to the others how Wotan incised this spear with the contracts and treaties in runes—by which he ruled and upheld the world (XI JUSTICE—WOTAN'S SPEAR). Recently, this spear was shattered by an audacious young hero, fulfilling Erda's prophecy that when Wotan's spear was broken, the doom of the gods would be sealed. In complete and despairing resignation, Wotan then ordered the dead World Ash Tree to be felled, cut, and stacked as firewood around Valhalla. She complains that she can no longer tether the cord of destiny to it—she must use a jagged rock instead. What will come of this?

The Third Norn describes how Wotan, surrounded by the other gods and heroes, now sits in a Valhalla that has become a virtual funeral pyre waiting to be lit. And when the World Ash Tree logs are ignited, Valhalla and the gods within it will meet their doom.

The First Norn nostalgically comments that the past was glorious—but it was so long ago, she can hardly remember it. She suddenly asks: whatever happened to Loge?

Winding the cord around her rock, the Second Norn answers that Wotan forced him to manifest the imprisoning ring of magic fire around Brunnhilde's rock.

Catching the cord, the Third Norn prophecies that Wotan will plunge his now-broken spear into the fire and ignite the World Ash logs with it.

The First Norn is distraught as she finds the cord hopelessly tangled. Alberich (as the agent who tangles the destiny of the gods) immediately comes to her mind. She asks what became of him?

The Second Norn observes anxiously how the rock is fraying the cord! She exclaims that their weaving no longer holds. She knows that the Curse of the Ring is undermining their work. What will come of this?

Plot Synopsis:
Twilight of the Gods

Upon catching the cord from the Second Norn, the Third Norn cries out in dismay that it is far too slack and must be pulled taut. But when she attempts to do so, the cord suddenly snaps and breaks! All three Norns shriek out in horrified distress, as the destiny of the world is now irrevocably severed.

Then, proclaiming that the world will no longer have any knowledge of their wisdom, the Norns sink deep into the earth to rejoin their mother Erda.

The scene shifts to Brunnhilde's rock, where she and Siegfried emerge from their sheltering cave in the full daylight (10 of WALSUNGS). Brunnhilde tells Siegfried she must love him enough to let him leave and accomplish his destined heroic deeds in the world. She has shared with him all the knowledge she possesses, including that of the runes. Remorseful that she has nothing more to give him, Brunnhilde admits feeling empty of knowledge and strength—but full of love.

Siegfried replies that he has not begun to absorb all that she has taught him. From now on, wherever he is, he will think only of Brunnhilde.

Brunnhilde admonishes him to think instead of noble deeds and acts. It is these that will unite them in the sacred flame of love.

Siegfried now gives Brunnhilde the Ring of Power, as a token of his undying love. He has forgotten its history and magic (as told by the Dying Fafner) and is ignorant of the strong personalities fiercely contending for it in the outside world. Brunnhilde also seems not to recognize this particular ring as the one Wotan informed her about before her banishment. In return, Brunnhilde gives Siegfried her horse, Grane. No longer having magical powers, he yet remains a rare and noble mount. If only she could be Siegfried's soul! Brunnhilde sighs. Siegfried assures her they are indeed one. And that they shall never part.

In the following duet of protracted good-byes, Siegfried describes Brunnhilde as "a radiant star." She in turn calls him "resplendent light."

I describe this moment—far too ecstatic to last—as "high noon in overachievers' heaven."

Once Siegfried has finally gone, Brunnhilde remains admiring her Ring (XV DEVIL—RING of POWER). The Ring is the unsuspected serpent lurking in this paradise.

Siegfried's Rhine Journey, an orchestral interlude often heard in symphony programs, accompanies the scene change. Beginning with a gracefully energetic melody, incorporating light, playful variations on the leitmotif of Siegfried's horn, the ominous deeper tones of the Fate motive increase as Siegfried approaches the Gibichung Kingdom on the shores of the Rhine.

4.
Plot Synopsis
of the Four-Part Ring of the Nibelung

Act 1

SCENE 1—
THE GIBICHUNGS LAY A TRAP

Gunther, biological King of the Gibichung Kingdom and his half brother, Hagen, are deep in conversation, while Gutrune, Gunther's sister, looks on. All three have Grimhilde as their mother, but Hagen has the sole distinction of the evil dwarf Alberich for a father.

Gunther asks Hagen what must he do to hold his head high in the company of the local dignitaries? Hagen, Alberich's willing tool, sighs that he envies Gunther his royal title. Gunther replies in turn that he envies Hagen's cleverness.

Now responding directly to Gunther's question, Hagen chides the King, saying there are certain things necessary to his high station, which he has not yet accomplished. For example, neither he nor his sister the Queen have found a mate. Gunther asks if Hagen has any suitable candidates in mind.

"I know of a rock surrounded by a ring of fire on which a beautiful woman sleeps, only waiting to be claimed by a fearless hero," suggests Hagen. Then he launches into the story of the hapless Walsung twins, Sieglinde and Siegmund, Brunnhilde's defiance of Wotan and her subsequent punishment on their behalf.

Gunther asks if he is equal to this task.

"It would take someone stronger than you," replies Hagen.

"Well who is there who could accomplish it?" Gunther wants to know.

"There is one hero by name of Siegfried, a Walsung, who could do it. He would also make a famous husband for Gutrune."

At this, Gutrune's interest picks up, and she asks Hagen what heroic deeds this Siegfried has accomplished. Hagen relates how Siegfried slew the dragon Fafner and won the Nibelung treasure, including a wondrous Ring. With this Ring he can bend all the world to his will and accumulate fabulous wealth.

A frustrated Gunther tells Hagen the discussion is a waste of time, if Siegfried is the only one who can claim Brunnhilde. "Why tantalize us with unachievable prizes?"

"But supposing," continues Hagen, "that Siegfried could win Brunnhilde for you?"

Plot Synopsis:
Twilight of the Gods

"Now why would he do that?" Gunther inquires skeptically.

He might, continues the crafty Hagen, (KING of GIBICHUNGS—HAGEN) if he were acting under an enchantment.

Gunther sputters in protest that he is completely incapable of such powerful magic.

Now Hagen pulls out his hidden ace: he tells Gutrune he has a potion in his possession that will cause Siegfried to forget any woman he had previously known, and compel him to immediately fall in passionate love with the first woman he subsequently sees.

Gunther thinks this potion is indeed a splendid plan; Gutrune, intrigued, wants to meet Siegfried. Just as Gunther asks how they might lure Siegfried to their kingdom, Siegfried's hunting horn is heard far off in the distance. Hagen tells Gunther and Gutrune that, as Siegfried is out in the world seeking adventure, he will certainly come down the Rhine and pass their shores sometime soon.

Siegfried's horn is now heard again—only this time somewhat nearer.

In response, Hagen rushes down to the shoreline and looks up the river. Fatefully, he sees Siegfried approaching in a boat with the horse Grane. While Gunther and Gutrune look on immobilized, Hagen seizes the opportunity, hailing Siegfried and inviting him to put ashore in the Gibich Kingdom.

SCENE 2—
SIEGFRIED IS BETRAYED BY HIS HOSTS

As Grane is led to the stables, introductions ensue. Gunther offers Siegfried complete freedom of his realm; Siegfried responds that while he has nothing but his sword, he pledges it to Gunther's service.

The scheming Hagen inquires of Siegfried, "But don't you also have the Nibelung hoard?"

"Oh that," scoffs Siegfried, who had forgotten all about it. "I left it back in a cave."

But Hagen presses him, "Didn't you take anything for yourself?"

"Just this piece of metal (XIV MAGIC—TARNHELM) which I haven't used," replies Siegfried.

4.
Plot Synopsis
of the Four-Part Ring of the Nibelung

Hagen then launches into a description of the magical powers of the Tarnhelm, finding it impossible to believe Siegfried is so woefully ignorant. Next he asks, "Is this all you took?"

"Oh, just a ring," is the youth's response. Barely able to contain himself, but trying to appear as nonchalant as possible, Hagen asks Siegfried if he has it with him. "I gave it to a wonderful woman," declares the innocent Siegfried.

Just then Gutrune enters carrying a drinking horn filled with Hagen's magic potion of forgetting (QUEEN of GIBICHUNGS—GUTRUNE).

In a supreme irony, Siegfried toasts his ever-faithful love for Brunnhilde just as he swallows the fateful brew! Immediately, Siegfried, looking at Gutrune, is seized with a consuming passion for her instead. He breaks out in a sudden declaration of love (PAGE of GIBICHUNGS—INNOCENT SIEGFRIED). An embarrassed Gutrune backs away leaving the men to themselves.

What are we to make of all this? Is it that purity and innocence will inevitably be deceived and twisted by the dark human egotistic obsessions for power, control, wealth, and revenge? That Siegfried, a demi-god and Wotan's grandson, is far too good for this wicked world replete with others' nefarious agendas, and that he will inevitably only crash and burn in it?

In any case, now completely under the spell, Siegfried inquires if Gunther has a wife. Remembering Hagen's suggestion, Gunther says he has his mind set on a particular woman imprisoned on a rock surrounded by fire. Siegfried repeats Gunther's description as if remembering something far off ... but after a few moments he shakes it off.

Gunther says the woman of his dreams is named Brunnhilde. Unfortunately, he himself is unable to penetrate the flames that protect her.

"Well, I'm your man!" Siegfried, too eager to volunteer tragically continues, "I'll claim Brunnhilde for you IF you grant me Gutrune's hand in marriage."

Gunther of course gladly agrees. Siegfried then lays out the plot whereby he'll use the Tarnhelm to assume Gunther's shape, brave the fire, and claim Brunnhilde for Gunther.

Delighted, Gunther calls for an oath: Siegfried and Gunther swear blood brotherhood, eagerly assisted by a silent Hagen. When Siegfried asks Hagen why he does not join them in their oath, Hagen responds honestly that his blood, being unclear, un-noble, and running too cold, would ruin their drink.

Together Siegfried and Gunther enthusiastically set off by boat to claim Brunnhilde as Gunther's bride. Hagen, licking his lips in anticipation of the imminent arrival of the Ring, is left in charge of the kingdom. Hagen has now pulled the strings on his two puppets Siegfried and Gunther. All serve Alberich the Nibelung and his son!

Plot Synopsis:
Twilight of the Gods

Another Orchestral Interlude delineates the next scene change. Primarily featuring woodwinds, it is tender and lyrical, descriptive of Brunnhilde in love. The music subtly suggests her vulnerability. It ends on a brief reprise of the "Ride of the Valkyries" theme.

SCENE 3—
BRUNNHILDE'S VALKYRIE SISTER DESPERATELY ASKS FOR HELP

Alone on her rock plateau, Brunnhilde is deep in a romantic reverie cherishing the Ring and her recent liaison with Siegfried (XV DEVIL—RING of POWER). Suddenly, thunder and lightning herald the approach of her ex-sister Valkyrie, Waltraute, on her supernatural horse.

Brunnhilde is ecstatic at seeing her sister and jumps to the conclusion that Wotan has finally forgiven her! She can't help telling her sister all that has happened: how ironically Wotan's punishment was a blessing in disguise, for she was awakened by Siegfried, the noblest of heroes, who has brought her the greatest happiness of her life. She joyfully embraces Waltraute who remains strangely unmoved and somber while listening.

When the enthusiastic Brunnhilde has finished, Waltraute tells her she is in complete error—Wotan has not forgiven her. In fact she is here in defiance of his orders on the gravest of missions and must speak quickly before she is missed at Valhalla (ACE OF GODS). Waltraute then recounts a harrowing tale of all that has passed at Valhalla since Wotan banished Brunnhilde. Ever since then, Wotan has no longer sent the Valkyries to ride to war. Waltraute describes them as a now completely purposeless and leaderless group. In addition, Wotan, in disguise, inexplicably abandoned Valhalla to roam alone in the world.

Anxious and distressed, Waltraute continues: recently Wotan returned with his spear broken in pieces! He commanded his men to fell the World Ash Tree, cut it into fire logs, and pile the former World Tree around the base of Valhalla. Then he retreated to his throne in gloomy silence, grasping his broken spear. He has even stopped eating the Golden Apples of Immortality! All the other gods are immobilized with anguish and terror.

Wotan has only been sending out his two ravens (2 of GODS) to report on the state of the world. Even when they bring good news, Wotan just smiles weakly. We Valkyries try to cheer and rouse him, but to no avail.

Then Waltraute recounts how, when she broke down sobbing in despair at Wotan's feet at this desperate state of things, he only remembered you, Brunnhilde! She heard Wotan say that if the Ring is returned to the Rhinemaidens, Alberich's curse can be lifted, and gods and men will be free again. Returning the Ring is all that can save the gods from certain doom!

4.
Plot Synopsis
of the Four-Part Ring of the Nibelung

Unknown to Waltraute is that Wotan has been wallowing in inertia at least partly because of remorse and guilt over his refusal to return the Ring to the Rhinemaidens when he initially had the chance. He feels responsible for the wreck of his own world in a selfish attempt to keep possession of it: for Wotan's theft of the Ring directly precipitated Alberich's curse.

But this is the ambiguous point: Erda in her pronouncement of the pending demise of the gods, never actually granted that the return of the Ring to the Rhinemaidens would forestall the end of the world. In fact the cause may be far darker and more obscure—linking back (long before the gold was stolen) to Wotan when he damaged the World Tree by stripping it of the branch from which he made his ruling spear. But in either case, Wotan acknowledges his responsibility in the crisis, even as it paralyzes him.

At this point, the belated return of the Rhinegold Ring seems the only course of action open to the gods that might just possibly save them. Waltraute certainly believes that it will. She entreats Brunnhilde to end the torment of the gods, lift the curse from the world, and save them all from certain doom (8 of WALSUNGS).

But guess what? Brunnhilde refuses to give up the Ring!

At this juncture, she cares nothing for the self-absorbed gods with their heroic entourage, who so willingly abandoned her to Wotan's harsh punishment. She reminds Waltraute that not only was she banished, she was also stripped of her immortality. No longer a god, she feels no connection or responsibility whatsoever to Valhalla—because of her holy liaison with Siegfried, she is now in effect a Walsung. Brunnhilde had, in any case, long previously withdrawn her loyalty from Wotan, whom she believed was weak and untrue to himself by acceding to Fricka's demands. Brunnhilde, in spite of Waltraute's ashen pallor, sees only flames in her sister's eyes.

When Waltraute protests that the Ring is causing all the world's problems, Brunnhilde replies that Waltraute just doesn't get it: the Ring means more to her than Valhalla and all the gods ever could as the radiant symbol of Siegfried's love for her.

Stunned by Brunnhilde's unexpected refusal, Waltraute realizes her cause is totally lost. When Brunnhilde orders her to leave and never come back, Waltraute rides off in distress.

The First Act ends with a truly terrible betrayal. Shortly after Waltraute's departure, the protecting ring of fire blazes up. Brunnhilde interprets this as the surprising imminent return of Siegfried. And she is correct in a manner of speaking—for it really is Siegfried—only now wearing the Tarnhelm, so that he appears as Gunther. When Brunnhilde does not recognize Siegfried as the figure stepping through the flames, she knows immediately that she is in dire peril.

Siegfried-as-Gunther, having had all previous memory of Brunnhilde erased, is there only to claim her as a wife for his new

Plot Synopsis:
Twilight of the Gods

blood brother. When she asks him who he is, Siegfried's heartbreaking response is "Gunther." A confused Brunnhilde, who knows that only the fearless hero Siegfried alone could have braved the protecting fire ring, tells "Gunther" defiantly that Siegfried's Ring will protect her. But Siegfried-as-Gunther declares that she'll soon marry Gunther with that same Ring.

A chase and pursuit of the fleeing and terrified Brunnhilde follows. But Brunnhilde is no match for the speed and strength of Siegfried-as-Gunther, and is finally caught. Brunnhilde emits a piercing scream as Siegfried-as-Gunther tears the Ring from her finger: she is completely undone. Siegfried-as-Gunther then forces her into the cave for the night. But he nobly places his sword between them to keep faith with the real Gunther for whom he acts.

Act 2

The Symphonic Interlude is a dramatic and gloomy overture (with a musical foreshadowing of the Rhinemaidens' warning to Siegfried) that sets a somber mood.

SCENE 1—
FATHER AND SON CONSPIRE TO REGAIN THE RING of POWER

This is a very dark moment in *The Ring Cycle*. It is after midnight when Alberich, who can now taste the Ring, approaches his son Hagen. Hagen confides his hatred of all others who are happy. Alberich replies that this is just as it should be, and that ever since that thief of a god Wotan was bested by one of his own Walsung offspring, he just sits depressed in Valhalla. Now they have nothing to fear from those troublesome immortals.

Hagen inquires who, then, will inherit the world?

"Aha!" replies Alberich, "We will!" That is if he can rely on Hagen to do his part.

He relates how Wotan's spear was split by the dragon slayer Siegfried, who now possesses the Ring, but who has never understood its powers. Siegfried is in love and far too happy! Together they will devise a scheme to destroy him and secure the Ring for themselves. Hagen tells Alberich he has already begun undermining Siegfried.

Alberich warns that in no way must the Rhinemaidens regain the Ring as that would be the end of all their plans. Alberich cruelly reminds Hagen that he was conceived for the sole purpose of helping him recover

4.
Plot Synopsis
of the Four-Part Ring of the Nibelung

the Ring. The Ring is the thing! He commands Hagen to swear his loyalty, just as the sun begins to rise. Alberich hastily leaves under cover of the fast receding darkness, bidding his unhappy son to remain true to him.

SCENE 2—
SIEGFRIED AND GUNTHER ABDUCT BRUNNHILDE

A buoyant Siegfried enters with the daylight. He is just back from his successful mission securing Brunnhilde as Gunther's bride. He used the Tarnhelm to instantly transport himself back to the Gibichung kingdom from Brunnhilde's rock. Hagen immediately calls for Gutrune and Siegfried to tell her he has won her for his wife. Siegfried boasts to Gutrune and Hagen how he braved the flames disguised as Gunther, and subdued Brunnhilde.

Naturally Gutrune wants to know what transpired in the cave overnight. Siegfried proclaims his honor by describing how he placed his sword between himself and Brunnhilde.

Gutrune next inquires how he was able to switch places with Gunther. Siegfried assures her it was easily done the following morning when they came down the mountain. Gunther and Brunnhilde are now returning via the Rhine in their boat and will soon arrive.

Just then the sharp-eyed Hagen sees their sail in the distance. Expectantly Gutrune asks Hagen to call the vassals together for a double wedding feast.

SCENE 3—
HAGEN ASSEMBLES THE VASSALS

Hagen, however, sends out the call for danger and all the vassals arrive with their weapons expecting to meet an enemy attack. Hagen tells them Gunther is about to arrive with a formidable wife. Assured her angry kinsmen are not following, the confused vassals ask why they are armed? Hagen orders them to slay sacrificial steer, boar, goat, and sheep for the altars of the various gods so the two marriages will be blessed. Hagen informs them there will be plenty to drink and that revels will abound. The vassals are highly amused to find that the grim Hagen has become a wedding planner.

Plot Synopsis: Twilight of the Gods

SCENE 4—
BRUNNHILDE ACCUSES SIEGFRIED of TREACHERY

Of course Hagen is spinning a plot: he tells the vassals to honor the arriving Brunnhilde, and that if she is wronged, they must hasten to avenge her. The vassals join in a rousing chorus as Gunther leads the subdued Brunnhilde, her head hung in defeat, ashore and into the square. While Gunther attempts to sing her praises, Brunnhilde remains sullen and remote.

Siegfried then arrives with Gutrune. Brunnhilde is electrified when she hears Siegfried's name announced. Tearing herself from Gunther, Brunnhilde engages Siegfried's eyes with her own, and staggers back when she finds no recognition in them. All the vassals wonder what ails her. Brunnhilde has been thrown into complete confusion at the sight of Siegfried—who inexplicably appears not to know her!

Innocently Siegfried asks her what is wrong. When Brunnhilde sputters his and Gutrune's name together, the simple Siegfried assures her she has it right—he and Gutrune; she and Gunther are to wed.

At this Brunnhilde explodes, and accuses Siegfried, "I married to Gunther? You lie!"

Siegfried rushes to catch her as she collapses. As he raises his hand signaling Gunther to attend to his bride, Brunnhilde is thunderstruck as she recognizes the fateful Ring on Siegfried's finger!

Now the confusion—and not only among the Gibichungs—really begins!

Hagen, having planned the terrible unfolding scene, tells the vassals to pay close attention to all Brunnhilde says.

Brunnhilde dramatically declares that the Ring Siegfried is wearing does not belong to him—it was stolen from her by Gunther. So how does Siegfried now wear it?

A confused Siegfried looks at the Ring. All he knows and says is that he did not get it from Gunther.

Brunnhilde demands that Gunther take back the Ring from Siegfried.

Gunther is also completely bewildered, truthfully denying ever giving it to Siegfried.

Brunnhilde asks him where, then, has he hidden the Ring he took from her? During Gunther's awkward silence, Brunnhilde puts the pieces of the whole deception together, suddenly realizing it was Siegfried himself in disguise who took the Ring from her.

4.
Plot Synopsis
of the Four-Part Ring of the Nibelung

But Siegfried, all his memory of Brunnhilde still blocked by Hagen's potion, defends his possession of the Ring, recollecting only that he won it fairly by slaying a dragon for it.

Seizing the moment he has so carefully and patiently orchestrated, Hagen "supports" Brunnhilde by saying that if she is certain that Ring is the same one Gunther took from her, then Siegfried has obtained it deceitfully and must pay for his crime.

Brunnhilde agonizingly shrieks, "Treachery! Treachery!" in the searing recognition that Siegfried has betrayed her and the holy love they shared.

Brunnhilde blames the gods for inflicting on her more terrible shame and suffering than anyone before her. She calls for revenge on her thieving betrayer Siegfried, who wrung a consecrated love from her.

Then Brunnhilde shocks everyone present by declaring that she is married to Siegfried!

A startled collective gasp is heard among vassals and the attending women. How can this be?

Siegfried (along with everyone else), misinterprets Brunnhilde's claim, assuming she accuses him of consummating their marriage the night the two spent in the cave. Consequently, Siegfried violently swears that he never broke faith with his blood brother Gunther, as his sword Nothung loyally separated them.

All those present wonder if Siegfried tells the truth. Hagen demands that Siegfried refute Brunnhilde's claim. Even Gutrune now has doubts about Siegfried.

The vassals insist that Siegfried clear his name by swearing an oath.

Siegfried agrees, and asks on whose sword the oath of truth is to be sworn?

The plotting Hagen offers his own spear-point.

Taking the spear, Siegfried demands that it strike him dead if he broke faith with Gunther.

Undeterred, Brunnhilde strides up and forcefully takes the spear into her own hand. She dedicates its power to Siegfried's downfall—may the spear kill Siegfried in just punishment for his perjury!

The vassal throng is now in an uproar: nothing has been settled.

Siegfried, attempting to save the situation, calls for a time-out. He tells Gunther to control Brunnhilde, who is a wild mountain woman and thus ignorant of Gibichung manners.

Plot Synopsis:
Twilight of the Gods

Aside to Gunther, he suggests that perhaps the Tarnhelm only half-worked and Brunnhilde somehow recognized him.

Siegfried then suggests everyone forget this ugly scene, inviting all inside to the prepared wedding feast—may they join in his marital celebration.

All file into the hall for the festivities—except Gunther, Hagen, and Brunnhilde. Absorbed in their private thoughts, these three hang back...

SCENE 5—
HAGEN SNARES BRUNNHILDE IN HIS PLOT

Brunnhilde, staring after Siegfried and Gutrune when they entered the hall hand in hand, is at first stupefied. Then, deeply grieved, she wonders aloud what "devil's cunning hides in this perverse turn of events, or what wizard's spell is at work." She is closer to the truth than she knows. Brunnhilde regrets lacking the wisdom she so freely gave away to Siegfried. She is stung by his easy dismissal of her, especially when she is in such obvious distress.

Who will offer her a sword to end it all?

Hagen the lurking serpent steps forward. He pretends sympathy for Brunnhilde by declaring he will take revenge on her betrayer Siegfried. But Brunnhilde practically laughs in his face: Hagen slay Siegfried? Never happen!

Hagen replies slyly that even though he realizes he is hardly Siegfried's match, the Walsung's perjury must not go unpunished. Hagen then asks Brunnhilde to advise him how Siegfried might become vulnerable to his spear.

At this juncture, I cannot help wondering how the curse of the Ring, which Brunnhilde once wore, might be fueling her searing betrayal, deep humiliation, and desire for revenge (2 of GIBICHUNGS).

At any rate, she freely relates to Hagen how she used her magic arts to spin a protective shield around Siegfried that no weapon can penetrate.

The wily Hagen probes a bit deeper, inquiring if there is any way at all in which Siegfried can be harmed?

Hesitating at first, Brunnhilde tells Hagen that while he can never be harmed in direct confrontation, he is vulnerable from behind. Because Siegfried would never turn and run from danger, she thought the charm unnecessary for his back.

4.
Plot Synopsis
of the Four-Part Ring of the Nibelung

"There my spear shall strike!" declares Hagen triumphantly, turning in the next moment to berate Gunther for his sniveling inaction.

Gunther responds self-pityingly, bemoaning his (supposed) betrayal and dishonor by Siegfried.

Brunnhilde voices her contempt for the cowardly Gunther, who hid behind Siegfried, asking the hero to win a famous bride for him. Gunther defends himself by admitting he cheated and used fraud—but he was the one defrauded and cheated in the end. He weakly appeals to Hagen for help.

Hagen pronounces that there is but one possible solution to both Brunnhilde's and Gunther's predicaments—Siegfried's death! Gunther protests that he and Siegfried are blood brothers. But Hagen rejoins that since Siegfried broke their bond of faith, blood is the only retribution. Gunther, suddenly unsure if Siegfried really did betray him, asks both Hagen and Brunnhilde if it is true. They both avow that it is so. Brunnhilde adds, more truthfully than she knows, that they have all betrayed her. She calls chillingly for Siegfried's death to redeem them.

Hagen now has exactly what he wants, and further baiting his murderous hook, he secretly tells Gunther that he can become an all-powerful ruler with the dead Siegfried's Ring of Power. But Gunther again hesitates, thinking of how his sister Gutrune will lose her new husband.

This incenses Brunnhilde, who believes Gutrune's sorcery to be the cause of Siegfried's unfaithfulness. Since Gutrune did offer the potion of forgetting to Siegfried, she is not far off the mark. Brunnhilde, however, does not suspect the scheming Hagen as the real mastermind behind her tragedy.

Hagen suggests to Gunther that they soften the blow on Gutrune by staging a phony hunting accident, complete with the fiction of a wild boar bringing Siegfried down. Brunnhilde and Gunther now concur that Siegfried shall die for breaking oaths to them both. The three sing a trio vowing vengeance in the name of Wotan.

Hagen exults in anticipation of wresting the Ring from a dead Siegfried and claiming it for his father Alberich—soon once again to be Lord of the Nibelungs and Lord of the Ring!

Act 3

The final act of *The Ring Cycle* is at hand! The action has moved from the town to the countryside, where Hagen's deadly hunt is in progress.

The Musical Prelude begins with the exuberant sounds of Siegfried's hunting horn, followed immediately by the dark,

PLOT SYNOPSIS:
Twilight of the Gods

ominous, threatening tones of the Fate motif. Yet a third musical shift recapitulates the Rhine music that began the entire epic. Finally, the lilting melody descriptive of swimming Rhinemaidens melts into their song of lament…

SCENE 1—
THE RHINEMAIDENS ASK SIEGFRIED TO RETURN THE RING

The three Rhinemaidens greet the morning sun, which only serves to remind them how dark their river realm has become since the theft of their Rhinegold.

The gold when it previously reflected the sun, lit their Rhine waters and infused them with life-giving energy. In their salutation, the Rhinemaidens petition the sun to send them one who can return their precious gold, "the star of the deep." Siegfried's horn is heard in the distance; their prayer has just been answered.

While tracking a bear whose trail he has now lost, Siegfried has become separated from the rest of the hunting party. As he walks along the riverbank talking to himself, blaming an imaginary elf for leading him astray, the Rhinemaidens rise up out of the river and greet him by name (6 of GIBICHUNGS). All four are in high spirits in the beautiful morning. Siegfried jokingly accuses the Rhinemaidens of luring his bear away—perhaps it is their lover? If so, he will spare it. They all join in laughter. One Rhinemaiden coquettishly wants to know what reward Siegfried will give them if they return the bear? Siegfried protests his pockets are empty. But another Rhinemaiden suggests he pay with the Ring he wears on his hand.

"Oh no," responds Siegfried, "I had to slay a dragon for this ring. No bear is worth that much." The Rhinemaidens persist saying he needs to be more generous to women. "My wife will scold me if I give this Ring away for so little," continues Siegfried. "Oh, will she beat you as well?" asks a Rhinemaiden. Again, more laughter. As Siegfried begins walking away from their river bank, the Rhinemaidens employ a strategy of flattery: speaking loudly so he can hear them, they describe Siegfried in turn as handsome, strong, and desirable (in nineteenth century parlance, "sexy"). But together, all three agree that "too bad he's such a miser." Then the Rhinemaidens dive under the water and disappear. This has the desired effect of drawing Siegfried back if only to protest being so maligned.

Siegfried in turn now employs a strategy of his own. He loudly proclaims he would gladly give the Ring to the Rhinemaidens if only they would return to the surface quickly. He removes the Ring from

4.
Plot Synopsis of the Four-Part Ring of the Nibelung

his finger, holding it in the manner of the proverbial carrot, high above his head. When the Rhinemaidens surface, rising to the golden bait, their mood has entirely changed. They are suddenly sober and serious, alluding to the dangerous Curse of the Ring. Replacing the Ring on his finger, Siegfried asks them to tell him what they know (XVIII MOON—RHINEMAIDENS).

They immediately inform him he is in grave danger, and that he keeps the Ring only at his peril. They relate the origin of Alberich's curse and warn Siegfried that as he slew the dragon, so will he be slain this very day! The arrogant Siegfried thinks this is all a joke and a bluff, and he scoffs at the Rhinemaidens.

They assure him they tell the truth. "Beware, Siegfried!" they continue, "the Norns weave the curse of the Ring into the rope of primeval law and world destiny every night. Only by returning the Ring to the cleansing Rhine waters can tragedy be stopped."

A skeptical and smug Siegfried declares he can easily cut the rope of Fate with his sword Nothung. Remembering how Fafner warned him of the Ring's curse, he tells the Rhinemaidens that as it never came to anything, there is nothing to fear. If only they had offered him love instead of these silly scare tactics and threats, he might have given them the Ring. But now they will never have it.

Exasperated at not being taken seriously and at how dense Siegfried is proving, the Rhinemaidens begin swimming excitedly in circles. They accuse him of breaking sworn oaths and of ignoring the secrets he possesses (the Runes). Furthermore, he was given a glorious gift (Brunnhilde's love) that he doesn't even know he has renounced! What a moron! He gives away what is most valuable, but keeps the Ring that surely dooms him.

The Rhinemaidens bid Siegfried farewell, leaving him to his fate (KNIGHT of WALSUNGS). Predicting that by the end of the day a woman will inherit the Ring—perhaps she will give them a better hearing—they swim off. Siegfried, in the folly of believing himself invulnerable, actually congratulates himself for his expertise on women! By ignoring the Rhinemaidens' warning and failing to recognize the truth when he hears it, Siegfried now steps fully into his ensuing tragedy.

SCENE 2—
SIEGFRIED AT THE FATEFUL HUNT

Siegfried is awakened from his self-congratulatory thoughts by the sound of Hagen's hunting horn. He answers with his own, and the hunting party, including Hagen, Gunther, and the vassals all arrive. When assembled, Hagen calls for a lunch break. Gunther appears extremely ill at ease. Hagen asks Siegfried to relate his adventures chasing game after he became separated from the rest of the party

Plot Synopsis:
Twilight of the Gods

that morning. All Siegfried found, he says, were three waterfowl who told him he would die today.

At this, Gunther shoots a meaningful look at Hagen. But Hagen, not missing a beat, suggests it would be an unfortunate hunt indeed, if the hunter himself were killed. Hagen then hands Siegfried his drinking horn filled with wine, and the thirsty Siegfried drinks. Hagen inquires if Siegfried can understand birdsong, as it is reputed? Siegfried admits that he has not listened to any birds lately, as his mind has been on women instead. When he attempts to hand off the drinking horn to Gunther, however, Gunther refuses to drink, saying he sees the blood of Siegfried in it.

Lightheartedly, Siegfried pours the remainder of Hagen's wine into his own drinking horn. Gunther—knowing what is to come—can't help admonishing Siegfried for being far too happy. Puzzled at Gunther's somber mood, Siegfried asks Hagen if Gunther is having trouble with Brunnhilde at home?

In annoyingly high spirits, Siegfried offers to entertain the luncheon party with tales of his childhood. He relates the story of Mime and his forge, of remaking the sword Nothung, of slaying Fafner the dragon, and of how, when he tasted a drop of dragon blood, he was able to understand what a bird told him. "Oh and what was that?" Hagen interjects. Siegfried continues saying the bird instructed him to retrieve the Tarnhelm and the Ring from the dragon's treasure cave, which he did. Then the bird informed him of Mime's murderous intent to kill him and claim the Ring for himself. After hearing that, Siegfried says, when Mime approached him with a poisoned drink, he promptly killed the dwarf in self defense.

Ever on cue, Hagen refills Siegfried's drinking horn, secretly mixing a magic potion of remembering into it. He hands the horn to the unsuspecting Siegfried, chillingly informing him that it will clear his memory—just so he will not forget anything. Siegfried drinks, but as he continues his tale, his mood suddenly loses its buoyancy and becomes noticeably more serious.

We now arrive at the crucial moment in Siegfried's recitative. The bird told him of a wondrous woman, Brunnhilde, protected by a ring of fire on a high mountain, who would make him an incomparable wife. Hagen, anticipating the moment when Siegfried will awaken to the truth and depth of his full betrayal to Brunnhilde, prods him to tell them more.

Siegfried goes on with his narrative of how he found Brunnhilde sleeping in her armor, how he awoke her with a kiss and then claimed her for his own; he describes how ardently Brunnhilde embraced him. Gunther is electrified by this new revelation. Just at that moment, Wotan's two ravens burst out from a nearby tree, circle above Siegfried, and then fly off. (2 of GODS)

Hagen, no longer maintaining his previous phony politeness, asks Siegfried in a brutal voice if he understood what the ravens just said.

4.
Plot Synopsis
of the Four-Part Ring of the Nibelung

When Siegfried jumps to his feet and turns to look up at the ravens, Hagen plunges his sword into Siegfried's back, answering his own question as he does so, "They cry revenge!" (3 of GIBICHUNGS).

The shocked vassals ask Hagen what has he just done? He arrogantly replies he has merely avenged Siegfried's perjury. Then he coldly walks away from all of them heading back toward the palace.

Meanwhile, Siegfried, in his last moments, finally remembers Brunnhilde as his true and holy bride.

The accompanying music, perhaps the greatest of the entire *Ring*, sounds a series of long, successive, dramatically tragic Fate motif chords—as the realization of how viciously he has been deceived dawns on the dying Siegfried. We hear many familiar musical leitmotifs woven together; then the orchestra swells to a powerful emotional climax as memories of Brunnhilde swamp the dying tragic hero Siegfried.

We experience Siegfried's excruciating struggle, as he continues on valiantly with his tale—but now nearly dead, remembering the moment Brunnhilde first opened her eyes and saw him, and then how she later laughed with delight at him.

Wagner's music here shreds our hearts in pieces—just as it is meant to do in faithfulness to Schopenhauer's idea that life itself will inevitably tear our hearts out—that in this world, it cannot be otherwise.

Siegfried's death scene was Wagner's original core inspiration for the entire *Ring* epic. He began writing the libretto (but not the music—that came nearly twenty years later) at this point in the story. I believe this scene conveys the electrifying emotional charge of his initial artistic inspiration.

Musical Interlude: *Siegfried's Funeral*

To the deep sounds of the Fate motif, the vassals slowly lift Siegfried's body and begin bearing it away in a sorrowful, stately procession. Night falls: Siegfried's light has gone out of the world. Gunther, the guilty accessory to the crime, hangs back, following the group of mourners at the very rear.

SCENE 3—
THE END of THE GODS

Later that night, back in the Gibichung palace, Gutrune wakes from disturbing dreams; she has been awaiting Siegfried's return from the hunt. Distracted, she vaguely remembers hearing Grane neigh wildly

Plot Synopsis:
Twilight of the Gods

earlier that day, and then—Brunnhilde's laughter. She observes a ghostly, unidentifiable form heading down toward the River Rhine. Gutrune calls for Brunnhilde, but gets no response. Throughout the evening, Gutrune repeatedly thought she had heard Siegfried's horn, but it was all in her imagination…

Hagen now returns, calling loudly and imperiously for the lamps to be lit. He proclaims that mighty Siegfried is coming home! Gutrune is confused, because she does not now hear his horn. Then the vassals solemnly carry the dead Siegfried in on a litter. Hagen explains to Gutrune that Siegfried had sadly proven prey for a wild boar that afternoon.

Gutrune throws herself across Siegfried's body. When an arriving Gunther tries to console her, Gutrune accuses him of killing Siegfried.

"Don't blame me," Gunther exclaims, "Hagen was the boar!"

At this, Hagen proudly admits that it was indeed he who slew Siegfried—the Siegfried who swore falsely on his spear. He audaciously demands Siegfried's Ring. But Gutrune shrieks in dismay that she, now his widow, should own Siegfried's Ring. It is hers!

In defense of his sister, Gunther attacks Hagen, and in the ensuing fight, Hagen kills Gunther. But as Hagen approaches Siegfried's corpse to tear the Ring from his hand, the dead Siegfried defiantly raises his arm straight up in the air in warning. Even Hagen is startled at this supernatural gesture, and he hesitates.

Just then Brunnhilde appears, proclaiming to everyone present that they have *all* betrayed *her*! Gutrune tells Brunnhilde hotly that she brought all this on herself. But Brunnhilde angrily responds, "You were never his true wife! I alone am Siegfried's rightful wife."

Suddenly, Gutrune realizes the terrible truth of how Hagen's potion of forgetting, which she gave so willingly to Siegfried, had erased all previous memory of the magnificent Brunnhilde from his mind. Gutrune now sadly concedes that Brunnhilde is indeed Siegfried's true love and consort.

Brunnhilde orders the vassals to stack firewood on the banks of the Rhine for Siegfried's funeral pyre. She offers a eulogy to Siegfried—how his radiance was like the sunlight—and how he was honest, loyal, pure. She invokes the God of Oaths to hear her lament! "Why did an innocent have to betray me, so that I could become wise? I hear the ravens stirring above; I send them back to Valhalla with dreaded tidings…"

Hagen looks on from the sidelines in horrified disbelief, as Brunnhilde now steps up to Siegfried claiming the Ring for herself. She encounters no resistance as she takes it from his hand. "My inheritance," she announces to everyone, "I give back to the

4.
Plot Synopsis
of the Four-Part Ring of the Nibelung

Rhinemaidens. May Wotan's ravens circle Brunnhilde's rock, and announce THE END of THE GODS!"

With that she lights Siegfried's funeral pyre and calls for Grane. Her single wish now is to be united again with Siegfried in the afterlife. She mounts Grane, urging him forward. They leap together into the consuming flames (QUEEN of GODS—BRUNNHILDE)—which subsequently spread uncontrollably, eventually destroying everything, including Valhalla. Thus the world of the gods ends in an all-consuming fiery conflagration....

All that remains are the River Rhine waters, which now wash over the burnt and smoldering wastes of that once glorious world. We catch a last glimpse of the swimming Rhinemaidens, who have at last recovered their Rhinegold, as they pull a struggling Hagen, still lusting after the Ring, to his death beneath their waters (10 of GIBICHUNGS).

The world, now purified by fire, can begin regenerating on a higher turn of the spiral. By committing a selfless daring act of immense physical and spiritual courage, Brunnhilde brings the old order to its pre-ordained end, setting in motion the next great evolutionary cycle on its cosmically appointed round (XXI WORLD—THE RING CYCLE).

PART II

THE CARDS
&
Divinatory Meanings

The **DIVINATORY MEANINGS** in this book are meant as a guide and beginning only; I do not propose them as exhaustive. It is my hope that those who use this deck will discover new layers, correspondences, and nuances in these cards.

Every different deck is a slightly different instrument with its own individual "tuning" according to Rachel Pollack in *A Forest of Souls*. Every individual Tarot card, in addition, can be described as a single note in a musical scale, each "having a different effect on the nervous system" according to Cynthia Giles in *Tarot: History, Mystery and Lore*.

So, if decks are musical instruments and cards are unique notes, is it possible to hear a spread of cards as a complete melodic theme? Such an analogy is especially applicable to *The Ring Cycle Tarot*, since Rackham's illustrations used here were his visual response to hearing Wagner's powerful music in live performance at Bayreuth, Germany. I have included the musical notes as ascribed to the trumps/Major Arcana by Paul Foster Case.

In this spirit, may these cards of art inspire you to wonderful divinatory music!

Trumps / Major Arcana

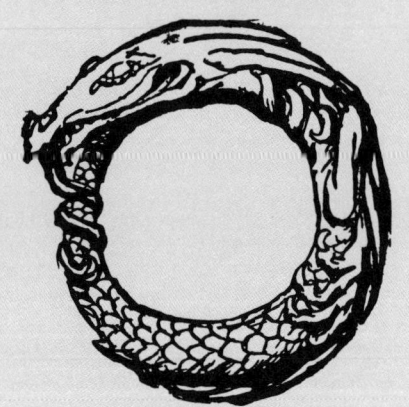

ELEMENT AETHER

These 22 cards represent universal human psychological archetypes applicable to all historic epochs and cultures, across time and space. Together, they can be thought of as a fifth suit of the Quintessence or Aether.

In readings, the trumps/Major Arcana carry more weight and "charge" than both the court and number cards: they indicate forces powerfully influencing events from behind the scenes.

The Fool
SIEGFRIED

(Siegfried)

"To teeming nature's store…add yourself joyously."

—Rainer Maria Rilke
German Transcendental Poet, 1875-1926

Musical Note: E

CARD BACKGROUND

SIEGFRIED has just reforged his father's sword Nothung in an act of pure inspiration. The sword had been shattered years previously by the barbarian Hunding in hand-to-hand combat with SIEGFRIED'S unknown father Siegmund, when Wotan removed its magical protection. SIEGFRIED now holds this sword high in confidence and sheer delight. He alone as the 'One Who Knows No Fear" was destined to make it whole again. Adding to his utter joy, is SIEGFRIED'S discovery that the dwarf Mime, seen crouching in the background, is not his real biological father as he had been told: SIEGFRIED now wields the irrefutable proof in his true father's legacy sword.

An orphan raised deep in a forest by Mime, far from the world, with only animals for playmates, SIEGFRIED has never even seen another human! Because of this, SIEGFRIED embodies the aspect of "the simple" fool who is pure and uncontaminated by worldly knowledge. Initially, this proves an advantage and a protection: everything is yet to be newly discovered and experienced without any preconceptions or complicating history.

With unnatural physical strength, fearlessness, and entirely without any hidden agenda or selfish motives, SIEGFRIED—FOOL acts here with complete freedom, elation, and abandon. Unschooled and untutored, he relies entirely on his natural good instincts to engage courageously, creatively, and enthusiastically with all he encounters.

Divinatory Meanings of the 78 Cards

Divinatory Meaning

This is a unique card in the Tarot: for while the FOOL dances on a journey through every other card, yet at the same time FOOL remains outside and above all of them.

My experience has been that when querents draw the FOOL, they often mistake it for a negative card that they think reflects their own ignorance and foolishness. On the contrary, the upright FOOL is generally an excellent draw.

It is the card of "beginner's mind," where we achieve success, just like SIEGFRIED in this card, without knowing exactly how.

SIEGFRIED—FOOL is descriptive of those rare moments when we truly "overreach" ourselves to create that which we never considered possible. It is a state of inspired Edge-work; it is "being in the Zone" of "Peak Experience." This trump reminds you to fearlessly believe that in this moment you are free!

Similar to SIEGFRIED, you feel confident and equal to all you may encounter, and you are ready to take on the world! The Unknown calls to you: freely answer. You set off now on a quest or a new pursuit in a positive "can-do" frame of mind. You are completely open to new inspiration and to new, even radical or revolutionary, ideas. Not being bound by conventional thinking can be a great advantage, both personally and professionally. This is the card of Scintillating Intelligence, shimmering with iridescence from Source.

You may also discover an unsuspected or untapped talent, or see a long-held latent potential finally take tangible form in the world for the first time.

Encountering SIEGFRIED—FOOL energy, you are truly being upheld and protected in the Light.

Reversed: This FOOL is another matter, and suggests, not only naiveté, but also recklessness, foolhardiness, and unwisely tempting fate. Here, your potential is not yet on solid ground. Overconfident, you may be failing to sense the real dangers in a situation that could be your undoing. Watch your step!

Magus/ Magician
LOGE

(The Valkyrie)

"Will the transformation…
be inspired by the burning flame."

—Rainer Maria Rilke

Musical Note: E

CARD BACKGROUND

In Rackham's illustration we see a LOGE who is not merely the half-elemental, half-god of fire, but a being *made* of fire. Fire, of course, is magical. Fire, like magic, is powerful and not to be trifled with. Both magic and fire can be unreliable and tricky—once set in dynamic motion, neither are easily controlled. Both are neutral forces that have potential for either construction or destruction.

The primal element fire embodied in LOGE is one of the great themes of *The Ring Cycle*. Fire is present in all four music-dramas as either forge, hearth, protective barrier, purification, or in the end, as a renewing conflagration. Wagner's scintillating "Magic Fire Music," which accompanies LOGE as he summons the Ring of Fire in this card that both imprisons and protects Brunnhilde on her rock, is second only to "The Ride of The Valkyries" in audience recognition and popularity.

In esotericism, all substance is described as containing a subtle "fire" of life at its core; thus, does fire pervade our entire manifested universe. In *The Ring Cycle* LOGE is a powerful exciting fire elemental and an amoral cynic. He never fully gives his allegiance to anyone. He distances himself from the other gods, thinking himself far cleverer; on their part, they are rightfully suspicious of him, as he finally proves the agent of their total destruction. LOGE'S relationship to Wotan is somewhat that of a manipulative court wizard. But Wotan on his part relies on the cunning LOGE to bail him out of his bad decisions and binding agreements.

Divinatory Meanings of the 78 Cards

1.

Divinatory Meaning

This is one terrifically powerful card! MAGUS—MAGICIAN describes someone who has the vital energy and dynamic will "to set the world on fire" through creative brilliance. This is the clarifying light of the fire element. While grounded in the flaming earth, LOGE'S gesture in the card is one of upward reaching, evoking, summoning; he then becomes himself the living conduit for the manifestation of these higher energies. Drawing this card means that you currently have available to you great powers of manifesting ideas and are bringing them through into form on the physical plane. The MAGUS is the card of the planet Mercury, indicating speed of thought, mental alertness, and ingenuity.

If this card turns up, think big and dare to imagine your heart's desire. MAGUS—MAGICIAN symbolizes inspired action, in which "Energy Follows Intent." It is a card of right timing, successfully manifesting natural magic, a by-product of "Transparent Intelligence" that necessitates utilizing the proper moment in etheric tides and energetic cycles.

Reversed: MAGUS-MAGICIAN sends a warning across your bow, for Mercury conceals a subtle poison. In reference to a person, be on your guard against someone who, while seemingly brilliant, is unreliable and will not "deliver," or meet your expectations. Beware of a charming con artist who may swindle you, either monetarily, intellectually, or emotionally. One commentator likens LOGE to a clever but unscrupulous corporate attorney whose sole loyalty is to the highest paying CEO (Wotan).

In the reverse, the MAGUS can be a person of genius with a history of mental instability, so look beneath this person's scintillating surface and verify their past history before placing trust in them. A current example of a reversed MAGUS-MAGICIAN is Bernard Madoff, who while purporting to be a "financial genius" proved instead to be an extremely cunning and deceitful criminal.

If MAGUS is descriptive of a situation rather than a person, the reverse suggests that creativity is now obstructed and the timing is wrong. Don't take risks, don't expect novel ideas to make an impact, don't look for any newly inspired results at this time.

High Priestess
ERDA

(The Rhinegold, Twilight of the Gods)

"... the Ancient, 'the root of what's been', the sources..."

—Rainer Maria Rilke

Musical Note: G#

CARD BACKGROUND

The prophecy of ERDA foretelling the impending doom of the gods is one of two events (the other being the dwarf Alberich's theft of the Rhinegold) that begins *The Ring Cycle*. In that world, both of these events are wholly unprecedented and entirely ominous.

ERDA is the mysterious Feminine Numen, the all-wise persona issuing from a deep fissure in the earth always accompanied by a mystical blue light (according to Wagner's stage directions). In this respect she parallels the mysterious underground vapors of Delphi, which the Oracle/Pythoness on her tripod inhaled to help inspire the divinations.

ERDA'S "dreaming," the basis of her life and her cognition, lies beyond time and space. Her daughters, the three Norns, translate this dreaming into the field of time by spinning it into the threads of individual destinies and the rope of world fate.

Dreams held great importance in ancient cultures. The Old Testament, full of dreams and prophecies is one good example of this. Temple Dreaming was a part of medical treatments in both ancient Egypt and Greece. There is a traditional Tibetan Dream Yoga and also a Toltec art of dreaming described in C. Castaneda's *Don Juan* books. The Norse put great store in "dreaming true"—presumably just what ERDA does. And Wagner himself used dreaming as an aid to composing: he claimed he was unable to devise the opening music for *The Ring Cycle*—until he heard the E flat chord sound in a dream during an afternoon nap.

Divinatory Meanings of the 78 Cards

1.

Divinatory Meaning

ERDA as the HIGH PRIESTESS embodies deep insight, inner illumination, and intuitive knowing. Immemorially wise, she embodies the mystical source of wisdom deep inside the Earth. ERDA (the German for "earth" is *erde*) is perhaps Wagner's operatic equivalent to the blind Schopenhaurean Will at work dreaming and impelling world destiny from behind the material veil. But contrary to the "brutality" of philosophic Pessimism, ERDA is neutral and unattached to outcomes—she intuits the whole greater cycle, the manvantara, and not just Wotan's brief part in it. Impacting *The Ring* world of the gods as an unstoppable supernatural force—ERDA'S dreaming can be at most only momentarily contained.

Drawing this card of the Deep Feminine indicates High Intuition and true instinctual discernment at work—either as a person or as a pure force influencing your query. ERDA, as Keeper of the planet's Power Points, represents the inner worlds of staggering insights. A prophecy may be afoot!

ERDA is the "Uniting Intelligence" of *The Ring Cycle*, connecting the densest aspect of the earth's core to its spiritual destiny, as well as giving birth to the Time Continuum through her three Norn daughters, the Past, Present, and Future. She embodies the Mystery of Ancient Planetary Memories and its Deep Wisdom, both of which are stored in our very cells and DNA. ERDA-HIGH PRIESTESS is the deepest strata of Truth. Now is the time to retrieve such knowledge as it is relevant to the situation/query.

Reversed: This card indicates your Inner Light is either outwardly blocked by an adversary or circumstances, or inwardly unacknowledged by yourself. You are not listening to or acting upon your Voice of Intuition or gut instinct. You see only surfaces, instead of discerning the causal inner substance and core.

III
Empress
FRICKA

(The Valkyrie)

"Sing the gardens you haven't known
…feel that the whole is meant, the glorious tapestry."

—Rainer Maria Rilke

MUSICAL NOTE: F#

CARD BACKGROUND

In his *Ring* libretto, Wagner does not create much sympathy for FRICKA, Wotan's wife and Goddess of Marriage. She is portrayed as a scold in a bad mood, intent on nursing her personal grievances. In the card, a very angry FRICKA races to "give Wotan a piece of her mind" and vent her disapproval of the incestuous twins Sieglinde and Siegmund. FRICKA of *The Ring* can be likened to a raging storm or bad weather that casts a pall on everything in its path. Everyone tries to avoid her (except the barbarian thug Hunding). Her husband, Wotan, no longer loves her, does not confide in her, and has sired these twins, as well as the Valkyries, with other women.

Divinatory Meanings of the 78 Cards

Divinatory Meaning

In a spread, EMPRESS—FRICKA indicates that the time has come for you to assert yourself and to make your point of view known to others, even if you risk unpopularity or disapproval in voicing your real opinions. FRICKA driving her chariot pulled by rams, the animal signature of fiery Aires, is a card of Feminine Leadership. Boldly step out of the pack now and declare yourself and your unique creative gifts. Rally and make a statement that cannot be ignored. While you may encounter resistance, you are more than equal to the opposition.

This EMPRESS also suggests embarking on some creative form building in your life. What project/s are currently engaging your imagination? Look for new ways to begin actually implementing and bringing them to fruition in the good Taurean ground of the material world. BE "the Luminous Intelligence" of living imaginative substance!

FRICKA of *The Ring Cycle Tarot* does not embody the luxurious beauty or nurturing energies of the traditional Empress; instead she upholds the harsher side of the Laws of Nature; she ensures that form, formality, and strict rules are adhered to and respected. She is the vital powerful life force at full flood. This EMPRESS embodies active feminine Mars energy rather than the quality of reposing Venus. Conserving natural law through leadership, she forcefully upholds appearances, convention, and tradition—especially the institution and sacrament of marriage—often at the expense of deeper feeling.

If this card is drawn regarding a legal matter, it indicates you may have a strong argument based on the letter of the law.

Reversed: EMPRESS—FRICKA is a powerful and passionate woman who may be unsympathetic, inflexible, angry and even self-righteous—someone who allows her own deep wounds to blind her to the feelings and needs of those around her. This card can indicate indulging in overly emotional or negative irrational states. It may also signify marital problems or divorce.

Emperor
WOTAN

(The Valkyrie)

"We make the world our own,
perhaps the frailest part, most full of danger."

—Rainer Maria Rilke

MUSICAL NOTE: C

CARD BACKGROUND

In traditional Tarots, the Emperor represents the archetype of the animus—the fully engaged male consciousness that is dynamic and powerful, in total control, reasoning and pragmatic, and one who upholds the Rule of Law.

In Wagner's epic, EMPEROR—WOTAN is all too human. He has managed to wrest control of the world, only to find it is not what he'd imagined: Wotan's powers are necessarily restricted by his own laws and treaties. Furthermore, he is trapped in a now loveless marriage to Empress Fricka. In both *The Rhinegold* and *The Valkyrie*, Wotan is a pragmatic realist—who "fudges the numbers" to get the results he wants.

The Ring EMPEROR—WOTAN is depicted in dialogue with his feminine (anima), his True Will. In this card, Wotan's beloved daughter Brunnhilde attempts to convince him to follow his heart instead of his head, and to soften his reasoned position with sincere and honest feeling. And while not successful, the feminine remains active and integral in this emperor's psyche—offering, perhaps, a truer and fuller model for all imperious rulers.

Divinatory Meanings of the 78 Cards

Divinatory Meaning

If you draw this card, it is foremost a directive to claim your own leadership abilities, as this is the Tarot card for the astrological sign of fiery Aires, the inspired administrator. EMPEROR—WOTAN represents authority and law, structure and order, responsibility and solidity. He is bound to uphold the status quo. This card can sometimes refer to legal matters or the necessity for legal action. It is important to remember, however, that emperors can often go astray and lapse into the extremes of absolutism, despotism, and tyranny.

EMPEROR—WOTAN can also represent the authoritarian patriarchy that now needs to redesign and rebalance its male world paradigm by truly sharing power with the Feminine.

Esoterically, The EMPEROR is "The Constituting Intelligence," suggesting he embodies the Laws of Nature by which the material manifest physical world is formed and sustained.

Reversed: A reversed EMPEROR—WOTAN has several meanings: you may be ignoring your own leadership abilities through fear of becoming a target. Apply the Spirit (rather than the Letter) of the Law, tempered with heartfelt understanding and compassion (that eluded Wotan). Lead and rule from the heart in addition to the head, honoring the Feminine Principle in thought and action.

Hierophant
BRUNNHILDE

(The Valkyrie)

"It is another breath that sings the truth."

—Rainer Maria Rilke

MUSICAL NOTE: C#

CARD BACKGROUND

In antiquity, hierophants oversaw Initiation into the Mysteries. A HIEROPHANT was responsible for "quality control"—examining the worthiness of candidates and insuring that all tests were fairly administered. Hierophants could be either male or female, depending on the particular Mystery School they served. They were also living reservoirs who preserved the Old Knowledge and ancient teachings, holding and transmitting this wisdom to the next generation.

In *The Ring*, the nine Valkyries, lead by BRUNNHILDE, initiate select fallen warriors into life after death to become the protectors of Valhalla, the residence of the gods. Only those about to die on the battlefield could see a Valkyrie. A high value was placed on this omen in the Old Germanic culture of war.

BRUNNHILDE demonstrates both the feminine Venus and the feminine Mars energy. In an attempt to fulfill Wotan's true will and inspired by her love for him, as well as love for his twins Sieglinde and Siegmund, she becomes, in spite of herself, a revolutionary. She refuses to obey Wotan's revised orders, because she believes they are contrary to his own heart's desire, and that he thus acts in error—for himself and for his entire world. At the crucial moment, BRUNNHILDE trusts her own perceptions and takes full responsibility for them. As a HIEROPHANT she claims her own spiritual authority and acts on her inner truth.

Divinatory Meanings of the 78 Cards

BRUNNHILDE is also ironically the "free hero" that Wotan thought he had failed to create despite great effort: the one who prevents Alberich from ultimately regaining possession of the Ring. Wotan, however, fixated solely on his male progeny, fails to recognize her as such. It is BRUNNHILDE who epitomizes Schopenhauer's assertion that the best that is possible in life is not happiness or bliss, but heroic struggle.

Divinatory Meaning

In a reading, *The Ring Cycle Tarot* HIEROPHANT— BRUNNHILDE may foreshadow an Initiation into the Mysteries, a change of levels, or an experience of a world new to us. The trump V HIEROPHANT is the card of "Eternal Intelligence"—the spiritual teacher within or without who counsels us to search for the higher purpose in our life experience, to discover truth transcending time, and to recognize the spiritual laws at work in all life.

While the HIEROPHANT is often interpreted as the teacher/teachings of a conventional church, BRUNNHILDE instead exemplifies the experience of direct contact with the living core of eternal spirituality, rather than its often calcified or crystallized sectarian and authoritarian cultural forms. HIEROPHANT—BRUNNHILDE instructs us that, paired with trusting the truth we discover within us, is *the necessity to act on it courageously in the world*. Belief by itself is not enough.

Reversed: This card warns of a betrayal. We may be betraying what we know, feel, and experience to be true for ourselves. We may be betrayed by someone we have trusted, as BRUNNHILDE is alternately betrayed, first by an enraged Wotan, and later by a bewitched Siegfried.

Lovers

SIEGLINDE AND SIEGMUND

(The Valkyrie)

"Nothing impairs the symbol that's true."

—Rainer Maria Rilke

MUSICAL NOTE: D

CARD BACKGROUND

This card depicts the archetype of the Sacred Twins, found in nearly every world culture. Examples include Romulus and Remus, founders of Rome; the Meso-American Hanaupe and Xabalbe, who defeat the lord of the underworld; the Greek discouri Castor and Pollux, patrons of athletes, immortalized as stars in Gemini; and Osiris and Seth portraying the ever-conflicting Egyptian ecologies of river and desert (water versus fire). This twin aspect is even encoded in the double helix of our DNA. Rare natural identical twins still hold a fascination for us.

SIEGLINDE AND SIEGMUND are the brother and sister twin offspring of Wotan by a human woman. Wotan helps raise these twins by masquerading as a human father of the Wolfe Clan, occasionally living with them as a family in the deep forest. He teaches Siegmund to hunt, hoping he will become the "free hero" he deems necessary to help him recover the Ring of Power. These twins are separated in early childhood when marauders attack their compound and abduct Sieglinde.

Divinatory Meanings of the 78 Cards

Divinatory Meaning

A romantic union or liaison, while generally the first meaning to spring to mind on seeing this card, is not the only one. SIEGLINDE AND SIEGMUND can signify many types of loving relationships or partnerships, as they represent the search for meaningful connection in our lives—be it personal, social, or professional.

In *The Ring Cycle Tarot*, LOVERS—SIEGLINDE AND SIEGMUND also importantly represent "Twin Energy": actual biological twins, twin souls (two people incarnating with the same purpose and having the same Soul and personality Rays), twin flames (two people with the same Soul Ray, but different personality Ray, who stimulate each other's purpose), or twin flares (whose Soul ray may differ, but who share a personality ray and who help one another shine more brightly in each other's company).

This card can also mean the discovery of other members of our own tribe or kindred spirits—those who share similar knowledge, outlook, values, circumstances, life experiences, or perceptions.

Most importantly, this card can indicate that an important choice now facing us must be made from the heart—above all other considerations. The Intelligence ascribed to this card is "the Disposing"—that which eliminates the nonessential and goes to the heart of the matter. Truly, this is a card of "The Path With a Heart."

And finally, LOVERS—SIEGLINDE AND SIEGMUND can symbolize the Alchemical Marriage of any set of polarities within our own individual psyche through the agency of Eros.

In *The Ring*, Wotan is forced to forfeit the lives of both SIEGLINDE AND SIEGMUND. Their ritual sacrifice, invoked in many ancient cultures for the good of the collective, is alluded to in their deaths. Because their forbidden incest violates the law of the land, the Sacred Twins must die. But Brunnhilde, acting against Wotan's (half-hearted) orders, does manage to save their unborn child, Siegfried.

Reversed: This card means that a connection in one's life is now broken. It could be one's romantic partner, one's sibling or other family member, or a professional or social friend/group. If in reference to the self, the reversed LOVERS indicates a severance from our heart's deepest and truest desire.

Chariot
GRANE

(The Valkyrie)

"Look at the sky.
Is there no constellation called 'Horseman?'"
Highway and turning. New vistas open."

—Rainer Maria Rilke

MUSICAL NOTE: D#

CARD BACKGROUND

GRANE, Brunnhilde's supernatural horse, like all the Valkyrie mounts, can fly between planes, dimensions, and worlds. GRANE is Brunnhilde's closest and most constant companion and, in the cards, she is rarely seen without him: when not riding him, she leads him by the bridle. GRANE even accompanies Brunnhilde into exile and is put to sleep alongside her; he too loses his supernatural abilities upon awakening. In many ways GRANE and Brunnhilde are one, exhibiting the ideal of strong silent love, loyalty, and unspoken telepathic communication between horse and rider.

Horses represent motive power, physical strength, and the force of pure instinct. We admire and respect that which remains wild and untamed in horses—perhaps we can even speculate on how GRANE may have added his own psychic fuel to Brunnhilde's willful rebellion against her father and King, Wotan!

A highly psychological aspect of the horse is its symbology as the "unpredictable outsider." This is also an apt description of Brunnhilde here and especially after her exile when, stripped of her immortal status, she defies the gods a second time by refusing to give up the Ring of Power, the symbol and token of her "marriage" to Siegfried.

Divinatory Meanings of the 78 Cards

Divinatory Meaning

Drawing this card in addition to all implied above, means a journey, speed, the Spirit of Adventure, the exhilarating Freedom of the Road. And not only in this world: GRANE can indicate a shamanic journey to other realms. This *Ring Cycle* CHARIOT also connotes a love of animals and an ability to communicate with them, advising you to hear and trust your "animal" instincts with regard to a matter.

Traditionally, CHARIOT is a card of Triumph and Victory, and represents strong forward momentum with regard to an issue. As "the Intelligence of The House of Influence," this card may also indicate a need for focus and directed will: hold the reins firmly and impose more control and direction in a situation, rather than being passively carried along by circumstances.

From an esoteric standpoint, Grane and Brunnhilde can be interpreted as our respective lower and higher wills. Ideally, the higher will of rider Brunnhilde will skillfully control the power of the purely physical body and its appetites, along with the ego-personality GRANE, so that through skillful guidance and direction, the broader and loftier goals of both soul and spirit can be achieved.

Reversed: CHARIOT—GRANE means delays in plans or expectations. The varied energies impacting a situation are not currently in alignment, so there can be no movement at this time. Use this delay to advantage by reviewing your strategy and preparations for the forward charge and the journey ahead.

Strength
SWORD
NOTHUNG

(Siegfried)

"Dance the taste of fruit…discoveries flow out of the fruit's flesh, surprised and set free."

—Rainer Maria Rilke

MUSICAL NOTE: E#

CARD BACKGROUND

In Wagner's third music drama, *Siegfried*, the title character, a young orphan demi-god, has just slain Fafner—the dragon who for several generations has been guarding the Nibelung treasure hoard and the Ring of Power. This is a remarkable accomplishment, since neither the cunning Wotan nor the scheming Alberich had been able to either outwit or subdue Fafner, in spite of years of furious plotting to regain the Ring of Power from him.

Siegfried is able to succeed in large part due to NOTHUNG, a sword magically charged by Wotan and inherited in fragments from Siegmund, the father he never knew. SWORD—NOTHUNG is initially Wotan's Hope, then Siegmund's Birthright, and finally Siegfried's Destiny.

Siegfried as "The One Who Knows No Fear," has reforged this weapon through sheer inspiration—not mastery or studied technique. He then uses it to make quick work of slaying Fafner.

In this card, Siegfried inadvertently licks a drop of dead Fafner's dragon blood from his hand, which instantly confers on him the magical power to understand the woodbird's song and to hear Mime's murderous unspoken thoughts. Siegfried, in effect, becomes temporarily clairaudient.

Divinatory Meanings of the 78 Cards

Divinatory Meaning

This trump describes an ability to summon either physical or mental prowess beyond your normal capacities and training to overcome previous conditioning. You raise your game to a new level. With NOTHUNG you approach a challenge with complete mental clarity unclouded by fear. You are now able to champion your interests and plans with great energy, inspiration, and motivation. Approaching a difficult task or test with a definite strategy in mind, you remain adaptable enough to spontaneously alter it if outer conditions suddenly change. You have the agility to "bob and weave" as circumstances dictate, and thus secure victory in your endeavor.

Traditionally, the Tarot Strength trump depicts the feminine powers of heart—compassion and wisdom subduing the (masculine) beast. For females here, young Siegfried represents the summoning of the inner animus/androgynous warrior mindset needed at this time.

STRENGTH-SWORD NOTHUNG confers the power to slay whatever dragon, either outer or inner, real or imagined, that currently obstructs you. Your hearing may now be unusually acute, and you, like Siegfried, may have the power to discern the truth masked by the words of others.

VIII STRENGTH is designated "the Intelligence of Spiritual Activities." Esoterically, this card describes the expansion of consciousness that can follow success in completing an Initiatory test.

Reversed: You are experiencing a failure of will or a lack of motivation. Perhaps this is due to being insufficiently prepared without a specific strategy. Back away from direct engagement at this time, as the odds of success are against you.

Hermit
WANDERER WOTAN

(Siegfried)

"Be—at the same time know the terms of negation."

—Rainer Maria Rilke

MUSICAL NOTE: F

CARD BACKGROUND

Wotan, King of the gods, disguised as a wandering human hermit, searches the world for information about the Ring of Power and his Walsung offspring. Since no one recognizes him as a god—much less as Wotan—people speak their minds freely. Wotan wears a patch over the missing eye he traded for a drink from Mimir, the well of knowledge and memory—one of three that waters the World Ash Tree.

In this card, WANDERER WOTAN enters Mime's forge and challenges the dwarf to a contest of wits. Mime wastes his only chance to find out what he really wants to know, arrogantly assuming that this hapless WANDERER could not possibly know the answer. By now, Wotan, having been forced to sacrifice three children, twins Siegmund and Sieglinde and Brunnhilde, recognizes the glamour of absolute world power as a futile trap.

Ever since the events of *The Valkyrie*, we see a Wotan, who, partly as a result of personal loss, has changed, deepened, and become the HERMIT—someone who seeks truth, wisdom, and understanding, rather than control or power. Wotan as HERMIT now comprehends that acting solely from self-interest is a dead-end.

But while no longer wanting the Ring for himself, however, WANDERER WOTAN here is still on a mission to prevent Alberich from reclaiming it and enslaving all the gods.

Divinatory Meanings of the 78 Cards

Divinatory Meaning

While the traditional Hermit is a card of one who has achieved spiritual attainment and Lights the Way for others, *The Ring Cycle* HERMIT speaks more to its prerequisite—the individual quest for truth—which may last lifetimes. WANDERER WOTAN here in his world search, embodies the Theosophic idea that "There is no authority higher than truth."

WOTAN in this encounter also reminds us that despite outward appearances, we never know to whom we are speaking! It is in our own best interest to withhold all initial judgments.

The *Ring* HERMIT, in addition, suggests the possibility that certain (metaphysical) Gifts have been embedded in the world by mysterious beneficent higher powers for us to discover and claim.

The number Nine of the Initiate refers esoterically to the transmutation of nine forces into higher energies: an initiate is one who has undergone an expansion of consciousness and is consequently receptive to different and higher frequency ranges. The number nine points toward secret knowledge and powers. Nine, the number of months of human gestation, is considered a magic number with unique properties in cultures all over the planet:

9 is the precessional single digit, as the length of each precessional astronomical age is 2160 years; and the length of 1 precessional degree is 72 years—which reduce to 9.

- 72 was also the number of days decreed for the ancient Egyptian ritual of embalming and burial.

- The Kabbalah denotes 72 names of God.

- The Mayan "Cosmic Number" of the Dresden Codex—1,366,560—reduces to 9.

- The Vedic Sri Yantra describes the 9 circuits of cosmic power.

- The ancient Chinese visioned a magic square of 9 on the back of the World Tortoise.

- *Star Trek's* ship *Enterprise*, with the mission to "seek out and explore new worlds" is identified by the number NCC 1701—a 9!

- There are 9 Muses, 9 Supreme Court Justices, 9 Valkyries, and 9 Worlds in the Norse/Old Germanic universe to cite a few more examples.

- Finally, a young pre-*Ring* Wotan hung upsidedown on the world Tree for 9 days, during which he discovered the Runes

The Intelligence of Will is ascribed to this card. The question for both Wotan and ourselves is which will do we choose to serve—the egotistical and self-important will or the transcendent will?

Reversed: A reversed HERMIT indicates that a period of intense solitude and soul-searching or an arduous search has come to an end. You may also now come out of hiding, drop your disguises and false personas, and freely cast off any social camouflage you may have been using for your own protection.

Divinatory Meanings of the 78 Cards

Wheel of Fortune
THE NORNS

(Twilight of the Gods)

"Oh, the splendid overflow of our existence, in spite of fate."

—Rainer Maria Rilke

MUSICAL NOTE: A#

CARD BACKGROUND

The NORNS are a variation of the Triple Goddess: Verhandi, a crone, is the Past; Urdhr, a mature woman, is the Present; Skuld, a youthful maiden, is the Future. Together they spin and weave the threads of individual fate into the rope of world destiny within the field of time.

They are the daughters of the Vala, ERDA (II HIGH PRIESTESS), a prophetic spirit of the deep earth. The flow of time is represented by the rhythm of the three sisters as they pass and toss the rope to one another in their work. One end of the rope is tethered to the WORLD ASH TREE (XX AEON), the living vertical axis connecting the three worlds of the dwarves (Nibelungs), the humans (Gibichungs), and the GODS.

Similar to the turning WHEEL of FORTUNE, THE NORNS depict a detached and relentless mechanism. As Wotan discovers, the NORNS have no power to alter or change anything: they must exactly spin only "the dreaming" of their mother Erda. While THE NORNS are certain that the Curse of the Ring of Power is somehow "bound up" with the destiny of the gods, they are ignorant of the details and specifics. For them it is just one of the many strands they are impelled to weave into the rope of the world each day.

This is the card of Destiny and Fate in the field of earth time. Today, we believe that we more or less create our individual destinies by our choices and actions, perhaps only impelled to some extent by our genetic and cultural inheritance, personal psychology, and astrology. In the old epics, however, from which Wagner devised his *Ring* libretto, one's fate was viewed as far more fixed and predetermined by awesome invisible powers working behind the outer appearances of the world (orlog or wyrd). In *The Ring*, THE NORNS according to commentator Anna Chapin, demonstrate "… the inconsequence of gods and men before the eternal Fate, which works its will against all power and all planning."

Divinatory Meaning

If you draw this card, the invisible powers of destiny are shaping your query in an exciting and dramatic way. Momentum with regard to an issue has been gathering force beneath the horizon for some time, and the result, often termed "luck," is about to break the surface of your life. There is no sidestepping THE NORN'S weaving, for once begun, powerful energies wind inexorably to their fated ends. Whether or not the turn of events will be fortunate depends on how you have seeded and sown the germinating circumstances up to this point. Assuming past sincerity, honesty, and good will on your part, expect fortunate change. Remember, however, that there is always the possible complicating tangle of past karma forming a knot—which must now be confronted—proving either helpful or impeding.

This trump may also mean that the moment is at hand for you to step into and claim your True Destiny in the world. If you are confused as to what this is, immediately begin some deep soul-searching inner homework, as THE NORNS, like time and tide, wait for no one. They are now giving you a significant life opening, so take advantage of this opportune time to take a risk.

Reversed: It feels as if the flow of time itself has been interrupted and events come to a standstill. In spite of your efforts, do not expect any change soon. This is not the time to risk! Assume a holding position for now. This is "the Intelligence of Conciliation" according to Robert Wang, meaning "the mediation of activity between rotating opposites" and (citing his Golden Dawn sources), "the counter changing influence of Light and Darkness."

Divinatory Meanings of the 78 Cards

Justice

WOTAN'S SPEAR

(The Valkyrie)

"Easy for gods to fashion."

—Rainer Maria Rilke

MUSICAL NOTE: F#

CARD BACKGROUND

Announced by a powerful thunderstorm, Wotan races toward the promontory where Brunnhilde, who has defied his orders, awaits the consequences of her action. The JUSTICE Wotan dispenses in anger can be truly terrible, inflexible, swift, and unequivocal.

WOTAN'S SPEAR, conducting the magical natural force of lightning, is the means by which he reigns and maintains order. In this card, Wotan is seen at the height of his power and glory, as lord of the world thundering out of the darkness, upholding written law and dispensing judgment throughout his realm.

Prior to the events that begin *The Ring Cycle*, Wotan tore a branch from the XX WORLD ASH TREE to fashion this great spear. (This act, however, at least partially set the end of his world in motion—for the gash he left on the World Tree became infected with a blight, which slowly killed it.)

As a means of concentrating his power, Wotan engraved all the treaties, laws, and agreements by which he rules on this spear. These are written in runic script—which, according to Wagner's literary sources, Wotan had previously discovered/invented only through great and intense personal suffering in a grueling nine-day Initiation.

"The Faithful Intelligence" is ascribed to JUSTICE. I interpret this to mean that worldly justice is invisible in the service of the higher order of cosmic spiritual law, to which it is ultimately ever faithful.

Wotan's magical/shamanic horse, the eight-legged Sleipnir, on which he rides in this card, symbolizes JUSTICE as a powerful, vital life force in its own right, even beyond reasoned argument. As such, it can prove unstoppable.

Divinatory Meaning

JUSTICE, necessary to social order, ideally achieves the correct balance of contrasting forces and opposing claims. The truth of a situation is the means of adjustment.

In a spread, this card indicates that the Rule of Law now supersedes all that is personal. Even Wotan is subject to his own edicts, though he might wish it otherwise. Yet while accountable for our decisions and actions, we do have the opportunity to negotiate, even as Brunnhilde subsequently does in an attempt to soften Wotan's fury.

Similar to a basic law of physics, in which every action sets in motion a reaction, so the universal law of karmic JUSTICE works itself out both within individual lifetimes and from incarnation to incarnation—truly, "we reap what we sow."

Reversed: In the reverse, this card reminds us that we have experienced or witnessed a miscarriage of justice that needs to be addressed.

Divinatory Meanings of the 78 Cards

Hanged Woman

BRUNNHILDE BOUND

(The Valkyrie)

"Don't fear to suffer pain.
Heavy are mountains, heavy the seas."

—Rainer Maria Rilke

MUSICAL NOTE: G#

CARD BACKGROUND

BRUNNHILDE BOUND is the Hanged Man of the traditional Tarot. The Ring trump shows her in suspended animation on a rock with the protective but isolating ring of fire (rather than the traditional element of water for this card) in the background. BRUNNHILDE has been sentenced to this punishment for attempting to save the lives of Sieglinde and Siegmund (VI LOVERS) in defiance of Wotan's (IV EMPEROR) orders. This trump is loaded with meanings.

DIVINATORY MEANING

Sacrifice is one important meaning for this card, and BRUNNHILDE does a lot of sacrificing throughout *The Ring*. She sacrifices her immortal Valkyrie status in an attempt to save her twin half-siblings and her father Wotan's "true will" as she understands it. To claim her own adult sovereign identity, she sacrifices her privilege and renown as the King's favorite. Later, she willingly sacrifices all her knowledge for the love of the adult Siegfried. Finally, she sacrifices her very life for the regeneration of her world. Sacrifice is meant here as an exchange of something of lesser value in the present for something of higher future worth—rather than the relinquishing of something irreplaceable one necessarily desires to keep.

Being suspended in a decision-making process, between acts, or in a holding pattern awaiting resolution, can also apply when drawing this trump, just as BRUNNHILDE must now, as depicted in this card, await a fearless hero who can awaken her. Here she represents the immobile suspension of the "the Stable Intelligence."

Another meaning of BRUNNHILDE BOUND is the concept of reversal—seeing a situation from a new perspective or adopting a different viewpoint about it. While your world may have just been turned uncomfortably upside down, things now do look different—leading you to new information, new ideas, new inspiration, and new strategies for action.

In esotericism, the "Reversal of the Wheel" indicates reaching a moment in developing consciousness when individual ambition for solely personal gain is replaced by spiritual service to the collective good. One changes direction and goes counter to the mass current in both thinking and in deed. The subtle inner planes have come to assume more reality than the outer world, because the unseen is experienced as the underlying deeper cause of the seen.

This trump can also indicate that a crisis point in one's life or in a particular situation has been reached. Something of extreme importance now needs resolution and can no longer be ignored. However difficult, it must now be dealt with. But be assured that once on the other side of it, a certain freedom from a new comprehension will result.

So another meaning of this trump is the idea of going deep within the core self to discover or retrieve something valuable—such as a forgotten memory, a solution to a dilemma, or an important key insight. (Long before the events of *The Ring* take place, Wotan, according to the old sagas, hung himself upside down on a tree for nine days and nights in a strenuous trial of initiation. While he suffered terribly, in the end he "retrieved" the magical symbolic language of the Runes as a gift to his world.)

Like father, like daughter. Here BRUNNHILDE suffers a painful banishment from the company of gods. But in the end, this deepening solitary experience strengthens her so she can free her world from its debilitating curse, effecting its renewal and regeneration.

Reversed: BRUNNHILDE BOUND indicates you have been unwilling to examine an issue in the needed depth. Instead of continuing to act in your usual way, stop, reflect, and readjust your course. By surrendering your resistance and changing your ideas, values, or point of view, you allow new energy, like a fresh, stiff breeze, to move a stalemated situation.

Divinatory Meanings of the 78 Cards

Death
VALKYRIES

(The Valkyrie, Twilight of the Gods)

"…we see our lives forever taking leave."

—Rainer Maria Rilke

MUSICAL NOTE: G

CARD BACKGROUND

In *The Ring* the nine Valkyries, daughters of Wotan and Erda, are omens and harbingers of death on the battlefield. They search the military camps on the eve of battle for the most courageous warriors and select them to be the Honor Guard in their afterlife for the gods at Valhalla. Anyone catching sight of a Valkyrie is fated to die heroically in the upcoming conflict.

DIVINATORY MEANING

The DEATH trump does not necessarily mean an actual physical demise, but instead poses the question: What have we outgrown and now need to release? DEATH in Tarot suggests "a great letting go" of something in the physical, emotional, intellectual, or spiritual bodies: we need to detach from past memories, ideas, and limiting beliefs about ourselves and the world, habits, negative patterns or addictions, relationships we have outgrown, material possessions, chronic pain—anything that has outlived its usefulness and does not serve us any longer. DEATH is the necessary katabolic astringent that clears space for something new to manifest. This card suggests that great and perhaps abrupt change—not necessarily of our own choosing—is upon us. Perhaps we are hanging on too tight?

Some Tarot decks rename DEATH as transition or transformation. Transition can imply crossing over to new territory, a new world, or being impacted by new energies. In *The Ring*, warrior heroes are transported by the Valkyries to another, more subtle dimension. In this way DEATH can mean a dramatic release from a restrictive condition or situation allowing us to engage in new worlds.

Transformation is the experience of our changing into something entirely different. We may use the old ingredients but, in transforming them, we end up with an exciting new mixture. We may not even recognize ourselves in this next unfamiliar, changed phase, so we feel unsettled and somewhat off balance. But this passes as an equilibrium replaces the old.

Just as trump VIII STRENGTH refers to clairaudience, so XIII DEATH VALKYRIES refers to clairvoyance, precognition, "second sight," or perceiving the cast white shadow of things to come. Call to mind the last instance in which you had this experience—is anything about it relevant now?

There are numerous physical deaths in *The Ring*, too. DEATH is inherent on all the physical planes. This includes psychological death to old selves as we outgrow them, the death of stars and galaxies, and the death-shift of timed cycles in precessing astronomical ages.

But DEATH is a condition on the form planes only, for, according to esotericism, consciousness itself may be conserved with training and practice, and not necessarily dissipated or destroyed at the demise of the physical vehicle. "Imaginative Intelligence," which we must employ to achieve the next new cycle, denotes this trump. Esoterically, death is viewed as the release of spirit from the confines of matter. In Wagner, it is said, DEATH is never an end, but always a beginning.

Reversed: DEATH-VALKYRIES suggests safety, security, and protection. You live to serve another day! Expect a continuation of something as it has been with no dramatic change.

Divinatory Meanings of the 78 Cards

Magic
TARNHELM

(The Rhinegold)

"The world changes as fast as cloud-shapes manifold."

—Rainer Maria Rilke

MUSICAL NOTE: G#

Card Background

The TARNHELM is a magical helmet finely crafted of metal by Alberich's brother, the dwarf Mime. It conveys the three magical powers of invisibility, shape-shifting, and instant transport. Wagner adapted this idea from the old epic sources he used that recorded the legendary supernatural powers of ancient tribal shamans. In Greek and Roman myth, Hades-Pluto, regent of death and the underworld, wore a helmet of invisibility—presumably to move about among mortals without being noticed—to find those whose time was up.

Alberich, wearing the Ring of Power, however, immediately confiscates the TARNHELM from its maker Mime and then uses it to become invisible, the better to spy on his slaves in the mines. The TARNHELM often changes hands along with the Ring of Power through the course of the epic.

While the traditional Tarot trump XIV is generally named "Temperance," Crowley in his *Thoth* deck, renamed it "Art" in reference to the Art of Alchemy. Taking the path of correspondence another step further, I have designated *The Ring* trump XIV MAGIC, because magic—like both temperance and alchemy—requires correctly blending the right proportion of the right ingredients at the right time.

The TARNHELM, as a magical implement, is itself an entirely neutral force: its results may be either good or ill depending upon the motivation and intention of its user.

Use of any magical item underscores the necessity "to get it right" and to cultivate "skillful means." Not only must we have these to effect magic in the world, but we also, most importantly, need to consciously direct that magic to truly worthy and selfless goals. Tragic folk tales of backfiring magic used for base ends by the self-serving or the unprepared are legion. This may be a clue as to why this trump is designated "the Intelligence of Probation." While we may be excited by the Tarnhelm's great and good possibilities for White Magic, the TARNHELM is unfortunately used mainly for selfish causes and unworthy ends in *The Ring*—by both gods and men.

Divinatory Meaning

If you draw this card, know that Magic is afoot! How might the magic of either invisibility, shape-shifting, or instant transport relate to the position this card occupies in your spread? Taking an imaginative leap, how can you positively employ them in reference to your query?

MAGIC—TARNHELM indicates you now have dynamic creative power at your disposal. It suggests tapping the new or previously unsuspected abilities that have suddenly become available to you at this moment: take time to identify them.

The MAGIC card also means you can call on the unseen, angelic, devic, or elemental realms to come to your aid. This can be a card of employing new strategies, and even, if necessary, of becoming invisible and of executing a sudden escape from an uncomfortable situation.

Reversed: If MAGIC—TARNHELM is reversed, you are experiencing a lack of magic, beauty, or power in a situation. MAGIC reversed is a clarion call to summon more imagination! As soon as possible.

Divinatory Meanings of the 78 Cards

Devil

RING OF POWER

(Siegfried)

"Night by night ... the ancient evil."

—Rainer Maria Rilke

MUSICAL NOTE: A

CARD BACKGROUND

The RING of POWER, the force of unstoppable temptation, obsession, and murderous corruption in *The Ring Cycle* symbolizes all the powers ascribed to the traditional DEVIL. The Ring exacts its terrible price on all who wear it and all who desire it.

The RING of POWER can only be forged from the XIX-NATURAL RHINEGOLD by one who willingly forswears all love forever. Alberich, the hunchbacked dwarf, taunted and humiliated by the Rhinemaidens guarding the Rhinegold, willingly struck this satanic bargain. The DEVIL thus tellingly enters the world, as Wagner has it, *through the renunciation of love*. Seeking revenge on his realm, Alberich claimed the gold's hidden potential for limitless wealth and world domination by forging the RING of POWER from it. Soon tricked out of his Ring by Wotan and Loge, Alberich retaliates by placing a murderous curse on it: whoever possesses the Ring will eventually be killed for it by another who covets it.

Some examples of the curse of the Ring:

- The giant Fafner kills his brother Fasolt for the Ring;

- Years later, Siegfried obtains the Ring when he slays Fafner;

- Mime, in an attempt to poison Siegfried for the Ring, is himself killed;

- Hagen, acting for Alberich, murders Siegfried to gain the Ring of Power;
- Brunnhilde takes the Ring from the dead Siegfried, and after her self-immolation, the Rhinemaidens reclaim it.

Thus finally is the Ring of Power returned to the Rhine, but not before wreaking havoc on an entire world and hastening its end! I think Wagner's message is clear.

Divinatory Meaning

If RING of POWER turns up in a reading, watch out! You are being sorely tested. The DEVIL may be tempting you to act contrary to your own deeply held inner convictions and beliefs—against what you know is best for your own long-term interest. This card represents, to quote Lon DuQuette, "all that lures us to self-destruction." In *The Ring Cycle*, it is all that perpetuates the destruction of the entire world as well. This includes environmental degradation fueled by fierce rapacious multinational corporate competition for natural resources, along with our hugely expensive technologically sophisticated weapons we can barely control. The DEVIL—RING of POWER represents our bondage to obsessions and addictions, be they drugs, sexuality, gold-wealth, power, revenge, or war.

The RING of POWER card may indicate any fateful entanglement we will long regret. It is any dependency that keeps us both physically and mentally enslaved, limiting us to action from our lower three chakras and blocking our Higher Selves. DEVIL—RING of POWER is black magic compelling our destructive desires for control, domination, and even (as in Brunnhilde's case) an obsession with romantic love.

This can be a card of secret vices for both individuals and the collective, especially with regard to Power/Control and Empire. The DEVIL is the Shadow we ignore that can unconsciously direct our actions. The RING of POWER symbolizes the vicious circle of injustice and consequent violence.

Yet DEVIL—RING of POWER represents "the Renovating or Renewing Intelligence"—because there is always the possibility of our breaking free and regaining our sovereignty if we can summon the necessary insight and will.

Reversed: If the reverse of this card turns up, thank Valhalla! You manage to avoid or escape the above situations. On consideration, you wisely decide to pass on a tempting offer (to "wear the Ring") and, if it is metaphorically already in your possession, you willingly give it up—saving yourself from certain misery.

Divinatory Meanings of the 78 Cards

Tower
VALHALLA

(The Rhinegold)

"When will the destroyer Time break the castle to shards?
…Ah, the specter of the transient."

—Rainer Maria Rilke

MUSICAL NOTE: C

Card Background

Wotan, who has wrested control of the world, is about to take possession of his new mountaintop VALHALLA, the gods' combined pleasure palace and administrative headquarters. The only access the gods have to this mountain stronghold is over the Rainbow Bridge—too fragile to hold the weight of either giants, humans, or dwarves. In the future it will be guarded by an army of the most courageous and daring human heroes in their afterlife reward for a glorious battlefield death. VALHALLA, the ultimate exclusive "gated community," seems impenetrable.

Below on the river Rhine, the Rhinemaidens, however, are clearly in distress, as they unsuccessfully try to get Wotan's attention. They demand that he help them retrieve their stolen Rhinegold. But Wotan ignores them, as he himself is complicit in the crime: he used the Ring of Power made from their stolen Rhinegold, which he obtained secondarily by theft and coercion, to pay the construction cost of Valhalla.

The rainbow replaces the lightning flash of the traditional XVI TOWER imagery as a portent from the heavens. While the rainbow generally symbolizes optimism and hope, in this card it represents false advertising for VALHALLA: all is not as it appears. What outwardly looks strong is actually fragile, vulnerable, and unstable.

For here's the fatal flaw: VALHALLA is really built, not on solid rock, but on Wotan's deceitful crime. In commentator Anna Chapin's words, "VALHALLA represents brilliant veneers beneath which there is only a vacuum."

Divinatory Meaning

If you draw XVI TOWER dramatic change is imminent. This could refer to outer physical circumstances, such as an unexpected relocation of a residence or job loss. Or it could mean a sudden shattering realization that completely reorders your thinking—and consequently your world. TOWER is the Mars energy of deconstruction and destruction. What you thought was entirely stable may perhaps prove to be anchored in a faulty or shifting foundation. Your sense of security is now shaken by such possibilities as natural catastrophes, incorrect assumptions, poor preparations and construction, or general instability in the greater field.

But you can also think of TOWER—VALHALLA as a liberating agent from a constricting situation that is too narrow and holding you back. Even if you don't feel adequately prepared or that the timing is right, events now force your entry into a new field of experience and perhaps a greater sense of adventure. This is "the Exciting Intelligence," electrifying a situation with a powerful energetic surge from beyond, like both lightning and rainbows.

In some circumstances, you may even think of XVI TOWER as a "prison break" and unexpectedly find yourself free. (Of course this might then entail the subsequent experience of "being on the run" too!)

Another relevant meaning is that of snapping awake from the trance of materialism. Just as the gods of *The Ring* are not saved by their exclusive real estate, you may need to revise your concept of success by replacing the super-competitive "Donald Trump model" and its big salary with such primary values as authenticity, finding joy in work-supportive relationships, and more creative time–if a smaller paycheck—instead.

In esotericism, the Rainbow Bridge symbolizes the Antahkarana, built from higher mental matter to connect each human with his/her soul. This bridge must be built individually by each of us, and is the means by which higher energies can flow into and spiritualize our physical and personality vehicles. In this context, The Rainbow Bridge is a primary connection to the divine spark within us.

Reversed: TOWER—VALHALLA indicates a period of calm and stability. A sense of optimism is well grounded and based on a solid foundation. You heed a timely warning and escape danger.

Divinatory Meanings of the 78 Cards

Star
FREIA

(The Rhinegold)

"Many a star was waiting for you to see it."

—Rainer Maria Rilke

MUSICAL NOTE: A#

CARD BACKGROUND

FREIA, the Norse equivalent of Venus or Aphrodite, tends the Golden Apples of Immortality. This fruit keeps all the gods eternally youthful and in perfect health. Without these apples, the gods would soon age, sicken, and die. Freia is a graceful maiden, whose beauty and generosity are also food that sustains—and not just gods.

Stars as far back into historic time as we can imagine have been interpreted as both the abode of disincarnated human souls, or—for the ancient Egyptian Pharaohs—the individual transcendent immortal soul itself radiating inspiration, hope, and guidance equally to all of us here on Earth.

STAR in Tarot is the traditional astrological card for Aquarius, the Water of Life Bearer. The incoming Aquarian Age offers us the opportunity to reimagine and renew our collective social and ecological vision for the Earth, much as the golden apples were used to rejuvenate the gods.

Divinatory Meaning

Hope and aspiration spring immediately to mind when STAR is drawn, as it is a card of possibilities for the future. At night we can bask in the direct radiance of the stars and absorb their stunning inspirational and revelatory energies. STAR can give us access to our higher minds, higher selves, and higher mystical intuition.

One way that astronomers categorize stars is by their color, and color allows us direct access to the soul.

A common belief is that we can follow our star, and tune into it for direction, guidance, and help. We also "wish upon a star" when we want to invoke the fulfillment of a personal desire. We employ stars for esoteric invocation and evocation.

STAR—FREIA is a card denoting both initial creative inspiration and the imaginative acts of beauty resulting from it. These "beautiful creative acts" include human interpersonal and collective generosity and sharing, as well as discrete works of art.

As FREIA is one of the youngest gods, another idea associated with STAR is that of inspired work with children or youth.

The higher aspect of Aquarius, attributed to STAR, is group awareness and group service, supported by attunement to incoming higher cosmic or stellar energies. In esoterics, a star is perceived as much more than an immense gaseous chemical reaction—it is considered as an entity with its own vast supra-human consciousness. STAR—FREIA embodies "the Natural Intelligence" inherent in all substance itself and by extension, our entire universe.

Reversed: A reversed STAR indicates torpor or ennui—a pervasive lack of energy and enthusiasm. What was once inspirational has now "grown old" for us. And while we may still have discipline for what we are doing, we lack the genuine passion for it. Or we are losing hope.

Divinatory Meanings of the 78 Cards

Moon
RHINEMAIDENS

(Twilight of the Gods)

"Voices, Voices. Hear."

—Rainer Maria Rilke

MUSICAL NOTE: B

CARD BACKGROUND

The three RHINEMAIDENS, Flosshilde, Vellgunda, and Voglinde together petition Wotan for the return of their Rhinegold. Their water realm, once illumined by the brilliant reflection of sunlight on their gold, is now dark.

This is probably the most famous of all Rackham's *Ring* illustrations. The depiction of the swirling River Rhine is a classic of the Art Nouveau style with its sinuous tidal currents suggestive of cyclic lunar energy.

The RHINEMAIDENS, graceful and beautiful aquatic creatures of pure instinct, become overconfident of their charms. By indulging in a thoughtless flirtation and letting down their guard, they allow the dwarf Alberich to steal the gold that illumines their world.

The RHINEMAIDENS, in addition to the Norns, can be interpreted as yet another variation of the Triple Goddess: the Dark of the Moon (Hecate/Crone) is the wisdom of the Past; the Full Moon (Mature Woman) is complete knowledge of the Present; and the Future coming into being is the waxing Crescent Moon (Maiden). Their united lament, heard periodically throughout the *Cycle*, sounds a note of warning that something is seriously wrong in Wotan's realm.

Divinatory Meaning

The MOON traditionally can mean a dangerous crossing replete with phantasms, illusions, and half-lights that can lure us seriously off course. Moonstruck, we can become hopelessly confused, tangled and lost within mental mirages. We forget our purpose. We lose our way.

The Intelligence assigned to this card is "The Corporeal," a description of the entire realm of the dense physical, especially our bodies. In the lunar regions we need to pay special attention to what our "gut" instinct tells us, as it is a far more reliable guide than the mind, which is subject to distraction, confusion, illusion, or delusion. How often has our body known, just as our mind denied?

The Ring MOON additionally suggests the need for restoration of something natural and important. The Rhinegold is crucial to the balance and survival of the gods' realm: without it a serious world-ending perturbation is set in motion. We might ask what, in our own world, does the missing Rhinegold represent? What has been stolen or co-opted that is necessary to our collective health and well being? What needs to be ecologically restored?

While a definite warning card for romantic liaisons, indicating unreliability, fluctuation, and shallow infatuation, the MOON can be a good draw for artists, poets, and therapists—those who investigate the multiple levels of the psyche and explore its depths with a clear goal and purpose. In this context, the RHINEMAIDENS can act as reliable guides, rather than as Sirens leading us into difficulties.

Reversed: MOON—RHINEMAIDENS are warning us of imminent danger: something or someone may prove unreliable. We are in a situation in which we are being "glamored" or misled in some way. We are not navigating correctly, or we've become distracted. For whatever reasons, we risk failing at our designated task. We need to stop, listen to what our bodies tell us, and reevaluate our planned course.

Divinatory Meanings of the 78 Cards

Sun

NATURAL RHINEGOLD

(The Rhinegold)

"More Light!"

—Goethe's Last Words
Johan Wolfgang von Goeth, 1749-1832
German scientist, philosopher and author

CARD BACKGROUND

Beneath the pristine pre-industrial waters of the river Rhine, the RHINEGOLD glitters and glimmers, reflecting the sunlight, and radiating the healthful, inspiring energy of joy and beauty.

Three Rhinemaiden water elementals (see XVIII MOON) are charged with its protection. The RHINEGOLD in this primal state maintains the balance of nature in the world of the gods. This card pictures a joyful realm in which nature and all its creatures maintain perfect harmony. The carefree Rhinemaidens dive and cavort in the sparkling waters of this "golden age" in untroubled moments of complete fulfillment.

Although THE NATURAL RHINEGOLD holds within it the secret potential for world power, domination, and wealth, it demands that anyone who would claim these "forswear all love forever." As *The Cycle* opens, the Rhinemaidens are over-secure in their false belief that no one could ever possibly make such an unthinkable trade-off.

MUSICAL NOTE: D

Divinatory Meaning

This card represents The Good, The True, and The Beautiful.

It is a state of sheer delight and pure joy, of being completely in the present moment in which "everything is here and it is good." XIX SUN is one of the highest energy cards in the deck. Think of it as pure sunlight. It is a resounding "YES!"

The meaning of this card is perfectly demonstrated by an anecdote of the Dalai Lama. During a teaching, a student asked him what the best moment of his life was. He unhesitatingly responded, "This one." The NATURAL RHINEGOLD is just this state of perfect clarity, presence, and harmony of being.

As "the Collecting Intelligence," the precious Rhinegold here gathers and then distributes the sustaining solar radiation to light the realm of the gods. In Rackham's illustration, it coincidentally resembles a fully illuminated pineal gland, believed to function as the organ of human—divine interface.

The RHINEGOLD in its natural setting symbolizes balance, wholeness, ecological health, high integrity, and inherent worth, which can apply equally to people, circumstances, ideas, and projects, or to a course of action.

XIX SUN is also a card of health and regeneration, indicating that a complete and full recovery will be made if there has recently been an illness or accident.

In a collective sense, it is a card of Group Work and World Service.

Reversed: A reversed NATURAL RHINEGOLD warns of over-optimism and overconfidence, and the necessity to guard your resources and what you value most carefully. (Don't assume, as the Rhinemaidens do, that the choices of others will necessarily be the same as your own.) Illuminating light may be blocked on any of the physical, emotional, mental, or spiritual planes; identify and examine the obscuring shadow.

Divinatory Meanings of the 78 Cards

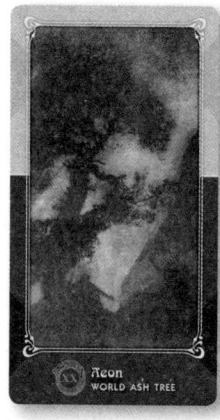

Aeon

WORLD ASH TREE

(Twilight of the Gods)

"We the endlessly risked, what eons we own!"

—Rainer Maria Rilke

MUSICAL NOTE: C

Card Background

This is the opening scene of the final *Ring Cycle* music drama, *Twilight of the Gods*. Time is fast running out for Wotan's realm of the gods. The light source in the card can alternately be interpreted as either the glow from the fire surrounding Brunnhilde's rock, the evening "twilight" (as in the title of this fourth music drama) or the dawn in the sky on the last day of the world. Perhaps it is all three, as we are now in Mythic Time, instead of linear, narrative time.

At this point in the epic, the WORLD ASH TREE, the vertical axis linking the divine to the deep earth core, has withered and died. Consequently, the world of the gods can no longer be sustained. This is Wagner's spin on the nineteenth century philosophy of Pessimism, as well as on the Norse and Icelandic end of the world Ragnarok scenario that pervades the entire *Ring Cycle*.

(I have chosen to use the concept Aeon, first designated in the *Thoth* deck for the XX trump, instead of the more traditional Judgment, as it better illuminates the meaning of deep time in *The Ring*.)

In this card, the three Norns are in dark shadow, having an extremely difficult time spinning and measuring the World Destiny Rope, which is now seriously fraying and, with mounting tension, will momentarily break completely. Why this must be so, the Norns themselves do not know and cannot say.

Implicit in this scene and in *The Ring* itself is the idea that even the gods and the Fates are subject to forces greater than themselves—forces imbedded in the very warp and weft of the cosmic space-time fabric. These incomprehensible mysterious powers orchestrating the Greater Cycles obscured at work behind the veil of our matter universe can be sensed, but not entirely known.

Divinatory Meaning

In a spread, this card indicates that *Time is Up*! The end of an important cycle and its succession by another and qualitatively different cycle is at hand. In our world, this is The Big Shift! A series of events, a particular mindset, or an important phase of a project or relationship/partnership is soon to end and will now assume a different profile. Experiences and energies relating to your query will be morphing.

This is "the Perpetual Intelligence"—in which the only constant is change!

Look to surrounding cards for more details on what form these changes may take, to what they may refer if you are uncertain, or how they may be implemented. If this card relates to you personally, you will be taking an important step towards your fated individual destiny.

If your query relates to a situation, AEON suggests that unknown powers are at work behind the scenes that cannot be altered. Destiny must run its course in this instance. But remember this can work in your favor! There is a new dawn at hand.

Because great changes are imminent in all cases, however, remain as open, flexible, and light on your feet and in your attitude as possible, the better to ride the winds of change as they occur.

You may need to move quickly with them. Embrace the future in lieu of fearing it by finding the opportunity in this crisis. When drawing AEON, adaptability in general and a willingness to make quick course corrections will prove invaluable in the near future. Vision a "new and improved" version of your circumstances or situation.

In the larger cosmic sense of a manvantara or a World Age, AEON relates to The Field of Time and our own last days in the cusp between the outgoing Piscean Age and the incoming Aquarian Age. WORLD ASH TREE further issues us a dire warning concerning our current ecological crisis of climate change.

Reversed: XX AEON advises that there is more to be accomplished with regard to a plan, project, or relationship. A cycle has not yet run its course. Your true path or destiny remains obscured at this time: more intention, preparation, and sustained focus are required.

Divinatory Meanings of the 78 Cards

World

THE RING CYCLE

(Post Twilight)

"We Die To Become."

—Goethe

MUSICAL NOTE: A

Card Background

Here is "Brunnhilde Transfigured and Risen"—*The Ring Cycle's* apocalyptic "Queen of Heaven" officiating above worlds, a resplendent Solar Angel. She symbolizes the radiant divinity within humanity, a Soul-Infused being, who has entirely subsumed the personality vehicle within a Greater Light. She has, now an Initiate, passed "through the fire, to the fire, and from the fire."

As an ascended World Server, she can now work with natural and spiritual law on the earth plane for the good of all beings. Brunnhilde of XXI THE WORLD comprehends The Law of Periodicity, implicit in *The Ring* and active in our own world, in which cycles begin and end in spiraling time, giving rise to yet other cycles ad infinitum.

Brunnhilde in this card has become the Evolutionary Agent who brings an old world age to its definitive end through the element of fire, so regeneration and "a bid for new and higher life forms" can begin.

Here is the question Burnett James poses: "If the world cannot be redeemed by a God with a spear or a hero with a sword, then who can redeem it?"

The answer is Brunnhilde—who, by acting out the Divine Feminine in the world, is the real hero/ine of *The Ring*—not Wotan or Siegfried. After a sudden blazing forth of the individual glory (QUEEN of GODS), Brunnhilde is now merged with the splendor of the greater whole.

As the esoteric Old Commentary describes it, "the jungles of experience are set on fire and dissolve in flames, and then the Path stands clear, and unobstructed vision is achieved."

Brunnhilde exemplifies Richard Rudds' Siddhic Rapture of Gene Key 30: by stepping willingly into the fires annihilating the collective past, she burns into a higher state of consciousness:

In XXI WORLD-RING CYCLE, Brunnhilde encompasses this unobstructed vision of the World Service Path. She here symbolizes *At-One-ment*—a complete identification with Soul Purpose and the Higher Divine Will, and embodying the higher spiritual aspect (enlightenment) of "the Administrative Intelligence." She has become one with the World.

Divinatory Meaning

If you draw XXI WORLD—THE RING CYCLE, it indicates that a holism—a dynamic and magnetic totality—has been achieved. Conditions for a renewal have been definitively established. This card can also suggest a clearing of some personal or world Karma.

Many energies on multiple levels are harmonizing, and they now all "dance" together. You are engaging with the Universal Light vibration in a unique and important, creative way—so make note of it! This card could also be confirmation that you have successfully passed an Initiatory Trial or Test of some sort. If so, share your success by celebrating your newly expanded view with friends and kindred spirits.

All systems, if not already reconfigured, are poised on the brink of a new equilibrium. In collective or group endeavors, this card signifies the triumph of high ideals. At the same time, it can indicate the possible need to surrender something personal for transpersonal gain.

Reversed: If Reversed, a cycle has not yet been completed, nor have all the pieces of a puzzle or a project yet come together. As a transcendent meld is not yet achieved, the next new level cannot be accessed now. Worlds may collide. More strength, stamina, and vision are needed to complete the desired unification.

Court/Royal Cards

King of Gods
WOTAN

(The Rhinegold)

CARD BACKGROUND

This is Wotan early in *The Ring Cycle* when he is consolidating his political power and world rulership. He stands behind the scenes, supremely confident that his strategies will keep him ahead of the competition.

He (and Loge) have come to Nibelhome for the sole purpose of stealing Alberich's treasure and Ring of Power. They need the treasure to ransom the goddess Freia, whom the giants are holding hostage in lieu of promised payment for building Valhalla, Wotan's palace stronghold. This outing, thinly disguised as a social visit, fuels Alberich's suspicions, but he egotistically demonstrates one of the magical properties of his Tarnhelm by shape-shifting into a huge serpent. He hopes in vain that this tactic will frighten away Wotan and Loge.

Divinatory Meaning

As King of the fire suit, WOTAN is symbolic of powerful, active, inventive male leaders of politics, science, the arts, or industrial-commercial entrepreneurs.

Wotan of The Rhinegold is a charismatic (though beleaguered) personality. In this card, he stands somewhat removed from the field of action, observing from a safe distance, awaiting an opportunity. He represents people with a compelling vision who are often empire builders. KING of GODS generally have outgoing personalities, are masters of networking, and are highly energized, canny, and savvy. They may well choose wealth, status, and power—as Wotan does—over love.

A variation of the KING of GODS can be that of an influential spiritual leader who effects great change. Of the four Tarot elements, fire is the least material and most symbolic of spirit. A good example of this type of KING of GODS is Ghandi: a leader who brought down a colonial empire by exemplifying the idea of nonviolent resistance and, who, while displaying a modest exterior, wielded an unbendable steel will fueled by an impassioned core interior fire for social justice and Dharma.

Reversed: A reversed KING of GODS describes a person of blind ambition, who uses his inspiration and creativity for mainly selfish ends. He can be a dangerous megalomaniac and a powerful adversary bent on winning at all costs. If this reversed God-King makes an appearance in your spread, think carefully before opposing him.

Divinatory Meanings of the 78 Cards

King of Walsungs
SIEGMUND

(The Valkyrie)

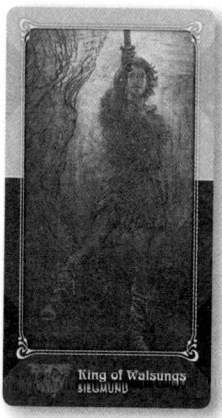

Card Background

Siegmund is a demi-god, the son of Wotan and a human woman. He was raised in the woods by Wotan disguised as the human "Wolfe." Wotan sired and then guided Siegmund to become a supposedly "free hero," employing the strategy that Siegmund would dutifully reclaim the Ring of Power for him.

Siegmund here becomes the KING of WALSUNGS when he discovers and claims the magically charged sword (VIII STRENGTH—NOTHUNG) and his previously unknown true name.

Divinatory Meaning

A KING of WALSUNGS is a man in touch with his feelings and emotions, one who has familiarity with and has no fear of his feminine side. Siegmund, of course, has the advantage of a "built-in" feminine aspect, in his identical twin sister, Sieglinde (QUEEN of WALSUNGS, VI LOVERS).

A KING of WALSUNGS is compassionate and humane, without being weak. He can be deeply intuitive and can excel at disciplines in the arts, or those crafts generally thought of as the sphere of women, such as divination. As a result, this King can be very discerning. He could be an outstanding musician or a renowned poet. A KING of WALSUNGS could very well be a leading world humanitarian, such as Jimmy Carter—a man who cares and mobilizes considerable resources to make a difference in the world. A KING of WALSUNGS acts from his heart, using his other great gifts (such as intelligence, social connections, or wealth) to support his focused feelings.

Because Siegmund dies early in *The Ring*, we never see his full potential realized as King. But by refusing Valkyrie Brunnhilde's offer to spend his afterlife in Valhalla without his sister, however, he demonstrates another trait of a KING of WALSUNGS: committed loyalty.

Reversed: this King could be someone wallowing in self-pity or overindulging in sorrow from disappointment in love. He may be letting his feelings and emotions prevent him from taking responsibility, needed action, or facing the future with resolve.

A male who draws a reversed KING of WALSUNGS, may have challenges with regard to the feminine principle in the world or within himself. If drawn by a female, a reversed King of Walsungs signifies a delay in romance.

Divinatory Meanings of the 78 Cards

King of Gibichungs
HAGEN

(Twilight of the Gods)

Card Background

Since Rackham did not illustrate Gunther (who is the biologic Gibich King), I chose HAGEN as King rather than Gunthur. Hagen, his half brother, is the true power behind the throne of the Gibich kingdom; Gunther does nothing without his counsel or advice. It is Hagen who deviously spins the crafty plots and sets them in action; Gunther is only the manipulated puppet.

HAGEN needs only a change of costume to perfectly embody an evil vizier from *The Arabian Nights*.

HAGEN, like Siegmund, (KING OF WALSUNGS) was also conceived for the sole purpose of helping his father regain the Ring of Power; both Hagen and Siegmund had human mothers. Only in Hagen's case, the father is the evil dwarf Alberich, rather than the God-King Wotan.

As KING of GIBICHUNGS—HAGEN represents the black genius. His ability to formulate and implement complicated strategies is formidable. But Hagen is pledged to the darkness: he shares his father's hatred and deep envy of all that is joyous, light, and free.

Divinatory Meaning

In a reading, however, the KING of GIBICHUNGS represents the intellect, the entire mental vehicle, and the power of concentrated focused thought. A King of the Element Air strategizes. He plans. He thinks things through. But unlike Hagen, not all KINGS of GIBICHUNGS necessarily direct their ideas and plans to evil and selfish ends. This card demonstrates that the mind is a tool that can be used in either positive or negative ways. We need to consciously choose how we use it. In *The Ring*, HAGEN exemplifies the tragically misdirected mind.

So it is important when drawing this card to determine who this might represent in your query, and exactly what the true motives of such a person are. If Hagen represents you, the querent, ask yourself how and to what you are directing your entire mind.

The KING of GIBICHUNGS always indicates impressive mental powers. But what ends do they serve? Who or what do they serve? We need to carefully discern the real agenda behind all this dazzling brilliance and not necessarily deem it valuable in itself. Great scientists, such as Kepler, Newton, Einstein, and Tesla, all exemplify positive KINGS of GIBICHUNGS, in that they used their minds as probing swords of truth or light lasers to delineate previously hidden forces shaping our world.

When we draw this card for ourselves, it counsels us to focus our minds and think deeply about a matter, considering it from all angles, similar to pondering a chess move.

Examine a course of action or other matter carefully for possible repercussions.

Reversed: A reversed KING of GIBICHUNGS is someone who may be over-thinking an issue, lost in endless permutations of plots within plots, or constantly replaying the same mental tape. This reversed King could be procrastinating, continually inventing new excuses for his refusal to act.

Divinatory Meanings of the 78 Cards

King of Nibelungs
ENSLAVING ALBERICH

(The Rhinegold)

Card Background

Here the dwarf ALBERICH in Nibelhome uses his Ring of Power, newly forged from the Rhinegold, to enslave his own kind: the dwarf and gnome earth elementals. He commands them to mine more and more gold and to fashion it into precious objects for his personal treasure hoard. His strategy is to use this wealth to build an army with which he can then overthrow the gods.

ALBERICH achieved his power of dominion (and consequent wealth) by swearing to renounce all love forever. This terrible oath is what allowed him to fashion the Ring, setting free the world's darkest powers. ALBERICH'S Ring of Power will soon poison his entire world.

This Ring exaggerates ALBERICH'S worst instincts and basest nature. As KING of NIBELUNGS, he seeks to exact restitution for an unhappy life by attempting to enslave his entire world. ALBERICH could be described as enveloped in a huge, untransformed, emotional pain body, as he is consumed only by hate and obsessive revenge.

The Nibelung realm itself is that of the Element Earth—dense, material, and mineral. KING ALBERICH'S native home is inside its caverns and deep mines, where light does not penetrate. In *The Ring Cycle*, the materially acquisitive and power-tripping ALBERICH embodies the most negative aspects of the earth element—hard, cold, impervious, unchanging.

Divinatory Meaning

In a reading, this card signifies that major issues of power and control need to be addressed. Examine what power is currently at the core of your life. Is it beneficial and invigorating? Or is it a cruel taskmaster? Have we become ALBERICHS, who have sacrificed all the love in life, only to become petty, controlling, selfish tyrants? Are we in thrall to selfish, materialistic goals?

Are we driving ourselves too hard in competition for wealth, status, and recognition? Or do we see ourselves unfairly enslaved by and at the mercy of an oppressive person or situation?

ALBERICH here can also be interpreted as Saturn, the astrological taskmaster, who imposes the restrictive rigor of matter and time. While we may very well feel oppressed, there are occasions when imposed discipline is necessary to accomplish our goals—perhaps this is one of them?

The KING of NIBELUNGS really poses the central question of the entire *Ring Cycle*: What in life do we choose? Is it power, control, domination, wealth, hate, and revenge? Or is it love of and service to the world through employing our highest creative gifts and talents?

Love and power are generally seen as mutually exclusive—this was Schopenhauer's view—from the lower self; Wagner's *Ring Cycle*, however, demonstrates that from the Higher and transpersonal Self, love really is power—in fact, it is ultimately the highest power.

Reversed: Through effort, imagination, and hard work, you liberate yourselves from deadening and painfully restrictive situations, both internally and externally.

Divinatory Meanings of the 78 Cards

Queen of Gods
BRUNNHILDE

(Twilight of the Gods)

Card Background

As I explained previously in "On My Card Choices," although in Wagner's *Ring*, Fricka—not Brunnhilde—is "Queen of the gods," for this Tarot deck, I have made FRICKA the Major Arcana III EMPRESS instead, and designated BRUNNHILDE as the feminine ruler of Elemental Fire. I have invoked artistic license in this designation, as BRUNNHILDE so clearly embodies the incendiary qualities of a Fire Queen.

Occurring at the end of *Twilight of the Gods*, this card paints the peak dramatic moment and culmination of the entire *Ring Cycle*. BRUNNHILDE, having reclaimed the Ring, leaps with Grane into Siegfried's burning funeral pyre. Her action spreads the fire, which in turn becomes the conflagration that consumes the whole world of the gods.

In the context of the epic, BRUNNHILDE commits a suicidal act; clearly she does not want to inhabit a world without Siegfried in it. Yet she remains at the same time the agent by which the Rhinemaidens regain their Gold. Through her daring last act, BRUNNHILDE not only removes the Ring and its curses from her realm, but also consequently clears the playing board for the next World Age to begin.

Here BRUNNHILDE is far beyond caring about herself. In this light, her irrational impulse may be viewed as self-sacrifice in the cause of world redemption. This is the theme of service and sacrifice of the lesser for the higher that runs unrecognized throughout planetary history, which Wagner so dramatically brings to our attention. The culminating moments of *The Ring* demonstrate the alchemical precept:

IGNI NATURA RENOVATUR INTEGRA

(Fire Restores the Whole of Nature.)

Divinatory Meaning

BRUNNHILDE as QUEEN of GODS is an "all or nothing" card; it indicates a person who is capable of full and total commitment, whatever the consequences. She has the courage of her convictions and is willing to pay the price. This Queen puts herself on the line for her deeply held beliefs. There are no halfway measures where this card is concerned.

The QUEEN of GODS can describe a personal apotheosis, a peak experience, or a blaze of glory, as it depicts a thrilling split second of pure transcendence. (The bill will come later). Such an experience could occur in the context of an initiation, or it could be an intense "trial by fire" experience in everyday life.

This Queen is a woman of daring action and adventure who combines these qualities with vision and inspired creativity. Queen Elizabeth I comes to mind as an historical real-life fire Queen of GODS.

In esotericism, this card is an apt depiction of "the burning ground," a freely chosen challenge and purifying crisis in which lesser desire and substance are burned away from the candidate on the spiritual Path. According to the Ageless Wisdom, "…before the Door of Initiation lies the burning ground which all disciples and initiates must tread—undeterred by pain." In the Wisdom there are successively difficult degrees of crossing "the burning ground," but they are all undertaken in consciousness and not in the physical world. The BRUNNHILDE of Rackham's illustration here offers up a stunning visual metaphor for this experience.

Uranus, the planet of revolution, is said to be a crucial active agent of these tests. And BRUNNHILDE is the revolutionary of *The Ring Cycle* par excellence on several levels, including acting as the fiery spark that ignites the world-destroying and regenerating flame.

Reversed: the QUEEN of GODS suggests you may be engulfed in the flames of a passion that does not truly serve you. Instead of making an impulsive leap of faith, hold the reins and pull back. Restraint is the best course now. Reassess a situation by enlarging your vision; strive to see the bigger picture. Conserve this high level of energy and passion for the time when it can make a real difference. Another reversed meaning is that you may not be ready for an impending challenge or test; if your preparation is not rigorous or thorough enough, this reversed card advises postponement.

Divinatory Meanings of the 78 Cards

Queen of Walsungs
SIEGLINDE

(The Valkyrie)

Card Background

SIEGLINDE is a demi-god and twin sister of Siegmund (KING of WALSUNGS). Like Siegmund, her early childhood was spent living in the forest with their father Wotan (disguised as a mere mortal), and a human mother. SIEGLINDE was kidnapped when raiders sacked and burned the family compound. She was then forced to marry the barbarian Hunding by her captors when she came of age.

This card finds SIEGLINDE an adult and Hunding's unhappy wife. It is night and Sieglinde is preparing a sleeping draught for Hunding, so she can speak freely to the mysterious stranger (Siegmund, her lost twin as it turns out, whom she has not seen in over a decade). He had sought refuge in their hut earlier that day when lost in the forest. SIEGLINDE, though not recognizing him, immediately felt a perplexing and profound connection with this strange man. The card shows her determination to discover why—even in the face of great danger.

Divinatory Meaning

All this demonstrates several important qualities A WALSUNG QUEEN possesses: that of deep intuition and the courage to act on it. These water Queens generally possess great beauty, especially when young. They are naturally nurturing, sympathetic, and compassionate. Often they are good listeners and wise counselors with regard to the feelings and emotions of others. A QUEEN of WALSUNGS has the capacity to perceive deeply with well-developed poetic and mystical facets of character.

SIEGLINDE as QUEEN of WALSUNGS has suffered much as a child and adolescent. In *The Ring* she could be the designated "Queen of Sorrows," as her life is short and tragic. While SIEGLINDE appears inwardly desperate in this card, when necessary, she can rally deep and great resources. (Later in the epic, thanks to Brunnhilde's help, she survives just long enough to give birth to a son, Siegfried.)

SIEGLINDE-QUEEN of WALSUNGS suggests that we embrace the feminine within ourselves, in each other, and in the world, and that we honor the Goddess in all experience and in all things. This may sound simple and easy, but it requires the courage and daring to take an unpopular stand and speak out loudly enough to actually be heard. The Authentic Feminine today in Western society is much like SIEGLINDE in her forced marriage to the barbarian Hunding—mute, subservient, and powerless before an unrestrained masculine technology that has become a new form of tyranny, continuing to fuel the cycle of endless planetary wars. (Many of today's high-ranking "poster" women have simply become males sharing in the spoils of power and wealth.)

Reversed: A reversed QUEEN of WALSUNGS indicates that we are discounting the Feminine and failing to see the Goddess by ignoring what our soul and intuition tells us. We lack the courage to act on our own truth. We may not be inwardly strong enough to meet the challenges ahead. This reversed QUEEN SIEGLINDE has conflicted loyalties and is not prepared for a full emotional commitment at this time

Divinatory Meanings of the 78 Cards

Queen of Gibichungs
GUTRANE

(Twilight of the Gods)

Card Background

This Queen, like Sieglinde, Queen of Walsungs, is similarly depicted with a magic potion in her hands. (Wagner often employed magic brews.) She has just filled the drinking horn with Hagen's Potion of Forgetting and is about to step forth with this poisoned liquid enchantment from the shadows to offer it to the light of the unsuspecting Siegfried. All this is part of Hagen's plan to regain the Ring of Power for his father Alberich. GUTRUNE is his willing, though ignorant, agent—she knows nothing of The Ring. It is enough that Hagen has promised her the handsome and famous Siegfried for a husband; all she need do is coax him to drink.

Divinatory Meaning

A QUEEN of GIBICHUNGS rules the mental plane and keeps her wits about her. She demonstrates purposeful ideas and thinking. She is clever, inventive, and enterprising. While there is nothing admirable in Gutrune's willingly drugging Siegfried (who she does not know is already committed), she thinks she is acting not only in her own best interests, but also in the best interests of the Gibich Kingdom. A celebrity husband will bring renown to the entire realm. So a QUEEN of GIBICHUNGS can strategize and institute long-range planning. She can wield her powerful mind as a formidable weapon to achieve her aims.

The traditional Sword Queen is often depicted as a spinster or widow, who may be experiencing deep and private grief. GUTRUNE, when introduced in *The Ring*, is something of a spinster and, after an all too brief marriage to Siegfried, rapidly becomes a widow. But in a sense she has always been alone, as the "odd woman out" and third wheel to Hagen and Gunther, who are running the Gibichung show.

A QUEEN of GIBICHUNGS is extremely capable and generally independent (much more so than the Gutrune in *The Ring*). As Queen of ideas and the intellect, she has a sword-sharp mind that can often probe patiently for the truth. She employs a finely honed edge of discernment to both situations and to people.

In this card, the GIBICHUNG QUEEN GUTRUNE is about to step out of the shadows and into the light. But to do so she may need to transcend her previous conditioning.

Additional meanings for this *Ring* QUEEN card include a possible "message from behind the veil" and/or experiencing interdimensional communication—a crack between worlds.

Reversed: A Reversed QUEEN GUTRUNE warns you that a pleasing appearance or façade may mask a deception or treachery. An intelligent woman with power who appears friendly and supporting may perhaps inadvertently betray you. To avoid disappointment or tragedy, carefully examine the true motives and underlying assumptions of this person before accepting any offer.

Divinatory Meanings of the 78 Cards

Queen of Nibelungs
GRIMHILDE

(Twilight of The Gods)

Card Background

"A woman bought with gold" is the description of GRIMHILDE given in Wagner's libretto. She agreed to bear Alberich's son Hagen strictly for money. Similar to Wotan in siring Siegmund, Alberich also engenders his son Hagen for the sole purpose of helping him recover the Ring of Power.

GRIMHILDE-QUEEN of NIBELUNGS is unhappy and remorseful: she has wealth and position, but no belief in her inner worth. Just as Alberich, the King of Nibelungs did, she abandoned love for strictly material reward. GRIMHILDE is pictured deep in a dark cave of Nibelhome, where no light penetrates. GRIMHILDE is also the mother of Gunther and Gutrune, but by a different father, the previous King of Gibich.

Divinatory Meaning

A QUEEN of NIBELUNGS is fully grounded in the world. Her red garment represents the base chakra, supplying the necessary energy, strength, and stamina to confront issues of physical survival. In GRIMHILDE'S case, however, she sacrifices her passion for life to obtain security and lacks the "juice of the grape" generally associated with a queen of the Earth Element.

Although Rackham has painted Grimhilde full of remorse, tinged with paranoia, the QUEEN of NIBELUNGS in a reading might represent a pragmatic woman of status and wealth. Successful professional women come to mind as representative of this queen—who may, however, have made irrevocable personal sacrifices, including their innate femininity, to achieve the corporate perks, status, and recognition conferred by a patriarchal society.

Is feminine leadership being sacrificed for (perceived) survival? Is the person in a reading to whom this card refers considering a Faustian pact?

Traditionally, this is an amiable, sensible queen with her feet in the good earth. Ideally, a QUEEN of NIBELUNGS can combine the best of both the material and soul worlds: fortunate in family as well as profession, she demonstrates a graceful ease (something GRIMHILDE of *The Ring* lacks entirely). This Queen has traveled far in life and outwardly achieved much—but GRIMHILDE poses the question—perhaps at what moral, ethical, and spiritual cost?

Reversed: GRIMHILDE-QUEEN of NIBELUNGS describes someone (male or female) who has "sold out." This person has sacrificed their highest impulse and their heart's desire, for whatever is easier, acceptable, and most financially lucrative. Someone who values comfort, respectability, image, and approval over their own authenticity and truth. This card reversed could also indicate guilt for a secret past transgression.

Divinatory Meanings of the 78 Cards

Knight of Gods

SPYING **LOGE**

(The Rhinegold)

Card Background

This card depicts Loge as the fire knight. He is listening carefully to the Rhinemaidens explain how the dwarf Alberich stole their Rhinegold, allowing him now to claim all the wealth and command all the power in the world. As the Rhinemaidens desperately petition LOGE to help them recover their Rhinegold, he spins a plot quick as wildfire—which he is.

This Nibelung treasure and the Ring of Power could be the very means LOGE has been seeking to bail WOTAN (III EMP and KING of GODS) out of his ill-conceived construction contract with the Giants for Valhalla. LOGE promised Wotan he would find a large amount of wealth equal to the originally agreed-upon price of the goddess Freia! LOGE schemes that he will be able to exchange the Rhinegold treasure for Freia and return the Ring to the Rhinemaidens afterwards. Everyone will be satisfied: Wotan, Giants, and Rhinemaidens. (All he has to do is take the treasure from Alberich.) But theory is one thing. Manifesting is another.

Divinatory Meaning

In *The Ring*, LOGE the Knight serves King Wotan, but he is not always a good influence. Like all fire knights, LOGE is fast acting, but extremely difficult to pin down. Similar to his element fire, this knight is changeable, shifts course easily, and quickly jumps from one thing to another. He can be charming and very inspiring, but he is not necessarily stable or reliable.

A KNIGHT of GODS may be charismatic, romantically exciting, and full of passion, but often his affections are not deep or grounded. He is easily bored and craves excitement. The KNIGHT of GODS cannot be domesticated—he needs the whole world for his playing field. But taken on his own terms, he can prove a delightful and scintillating comrade and companion (think short-term, being in the moment, and/or no commitments).

James Bond, the fictional British spy, is a good equivalent for LOGE here, who acts as Wotan's intelligence agent in this card.

If this card is read in reference to the querent, it counsels careful listening—and then taking quick action, even though the end results may have an unexpected twist!

Reversed: A reversed KNIGHT of GODS warns us not to reveal information that can be misused by others for their own agendas. Do not count on a reversed KNIGHT of GODS for rescue or sustained loyalty.

Divinatory Meanings of the 78 Cards

Knight of Walsungs
SIEGFRIED

(Twilight of The Gods)

Card Background

Siegfried as KNIGHT of WALSUNGS, is engaging in conversation with the Rhinemaidens in *Twilight of the Gods*. He has been separated from the rest of Hagen's hunting party in pursuit of elusive prey. Hailing the hero, the Rhinemaidens hope to cajole him into returning the Ring of Power. But when Siegfried refuses, their mood darkens and they soberly warn him that he will be the next victim of the Curse of the Ring this very day!

KNIGHT SIEGFRIED, however, in a playful, buoyant mood, enjoying himself in the day's hunt, is dangerously overconfident. He cannot remotely entertain any possibility of the terrible tragedy about to engulf him. He suspiciously discounts the Rhinemaidens' warning as a transparent attempt to manipulate him, first through flirtation and then through fear.

WALSUNGS is the suit of feelings and the emotions. In *The Ring Cycle*, SIEGFRIED, who has grown up as a solitary in the deep forest, navigates the world purely on his instincts and his feelings. He has not yet learned to apply any real analysis to situations—he simply powers through them. And, until this moment, with the exception of Hagen's potion, such an approach has seemingly worked splendidly.

The Rhinemaidens here offer SIEGFRIED the chance to save himself, if not his world. He, however, proves the proverbial naive reversed FOOL by refusing to take both them and their warning seriously.

Divinatory Meaning

Due to inexperience, idealistic and romantic young water knights may project their high ideals unrealistically onto those around them. SIEGFRIED does so fatally in his dealings with the Gibichungs. Though SIEGFRIED of *The Ring* is generally outgoing, energetic, and exuberant, we can easily believe that, similar to many water knights, he also possesses a dreamy and poetic side. Singer-songwriters often exemplify KNIGHT of WALSUNGS/CUPS. Women generally find these sensitive, compassionate, and caring troubadours very attractive—at least for a time.

But a lack of worldliness can be the undoing of these knights. So it proves with Siegfried.

The KNIGHT of WALSUNGS is yet another card telling us to listen carefully to a message or warning from the Feminine, perhaps near water.

The Rhinemaidens here ask Knight Siegfried for his help; if you are similarly being asked for yours, it is in your best interest to respond with generosity. Heed a request to return to its rightful owner anything you may have borrowed.

This is one of *The Ring*'s pivotal dramatic moments—for if SIEGFRIED had returned The Ring as the Rhinemaidens had requested here, Hagen would then have lost his motive for murdering him in the next scene. And just possibly, the world of the gods might have endured.

One of the recurring themes of *The Ring* is that men ignore at their dire peril feminine knowledge, wisdom, and warnings.

Reversed: A reversed KNIGHT of WALSUNGS/CUPS, may be a person trying, similar to water, to fill and assume the shapes and forms others suggest or provide for him, rather than discovering his own authentic form for himself. This Knight needs more solidity as a counterpoise to all his lovely fluidity. A strain of narcissism may also color a KNIGHT of WALSUNGS in that sometimes he can become lost and completely self-absorbed in his own watery reflection.

Divinatory Meanings of the 78 Cards

Knight of Gibichungs
AVENGING ALBERICH

(The Rhinegold)

Card Background

ALBERICH the dwarf, whose theft of the Rhinegold begins *The Ring Cycle*, proves not only capable of renouncing all love forever in exchange for wealth and power, but also never entertains a single regret over this decision—even though it condemns him to a life of painful, emotional isolation and mental misery. KNIGHT AVENGING ALBERICH is Wotan's polar opposite, and these two symbolize the ongoing battle in the world between the dual forces of preservation and destruction. Wotan knows full well he has met his adversarial match in ALBERICH, his dark rebellious knight: ALBERICH announces his plan to bring down Wotan's kingdom and enslave all the gods.

However distorted and negative ALBERICH'S thinking is, it is nonetheless an extremely powerful force that must be confronted and countered—and not only in *The Ring Cycle*.

ALBERICH can be considered the dynamic force of mass negative thinking and nihilism active today in our world. He is representative of humanity's collective pain body that threatens our destruction by preventing us from utilizing our sustained collective thought to vision a positive future for ourselves and our planet.

Divinatory Meaning

The Nibelung dwarf Knight ALBERICH represents the dangerous narcissistic power of intelligence without love, and technology without heart—both narrow ends in themselves that do not serve the greater human and planetary good.

In a spread, however, KNIGHT AVENGING ALBERICH on a gold-colored background indicates that the moment is at hand to summon all your ideas, mental powers, and dynamic will, mobilizing them to advance your own interests. You can make a forceful, even confrontational, move at this time. Seize the day! Currently your mental energy is at peak strength, so direct it to positive ends. Express yourself and communicate. Here is a golden moment to move yourself and your ideas forward. Keep in mind, though, that your progress needs to benefit others as well as yourself.

This powerfully energized opportunity is short-lived, so act swiftly.

Reversed: Knight ALBERICH, as a dark Knight, represents a powerful adversary or opposing energy that now blocks your progress. There is strong opposition to your ideas and beliefs, so it is not the time to act on them. Keep your ideas to yourself, maintain a low profile, carefully fly under the radar, and bide your time until conditions improve.

Divinatory Meanings of the 78 Cards

Knight of Nibelungs

BLACKSMITH **MIME**

(Siegfried)

Card Background

The dwarf MIME, Alberich's brother, works away in his forest forge in Wagner's third music drama *Siegfried*. He is the master metal craftsman who created the magical XIV TARNHELM, yet he seems to have no sense of accomplishment or self-worth. Like Wotan and Alberich, he has become singularly obsessed with the Ring of Power, scheming away how he can obtain it while he works.

In this card, Mime forges yet another sword for his orphan ward, Siegfried, now a young adult, whose uncanny strength shatters every blade MIME'S great skill can devise.

Divinatory Meaning

In a spread, MIME as the Earth KNIGHT of NIBELUNGS symbolizes both the *will to form* and the *forming process* on the material plane. He represents creative gifts, mastery, skill, artisanship, as well as Magical Work. This card also denotes the concentration, focus, attention to detail, and sheer hard work necessary to achieve all these. This KNIGHT is concerned with the process of "hammering out the details" of a creative project or an agreement. This is a card of engaging meaningful work, well suited to your talents.

There is, however, the danger here of becoming over-committed to a too narrow idea of the finished product, so that the joyful élan is crushed, and no advantage is taken of serendipitous accidents that may actually greatly enliven the final result.

Drawing this card could indicate that you, like the sword, are being tempered and forged in a somewhat painful event related to the material plane concerns of employment, finances, or residence. But in the end, any "tempering" you endure may actually work to your advantage in an unforeseen and surprising way.

Reversed: this KNIGHT OF NIBELUNGS tells us we are not using your creative gifts to their full advantage. We may have lost the inspiration we need to "push through" to finish a project. It's time to rekindle our interest in it. Is someone else taking credit for our work, or unfairly capitalizing on it?

Divinatory Meanings of the 78 Cards

Page of Gods

THOR

(The Rhinegold)

Card Background

At the end of the first music drama, *The Rhinegold*, THOR summons his strength and throws his hammer to create the Rainbow Bridge, providing Wotan and all the gods access to Valhalla, their newly built home on the lofty mountain heights. The gods are in a jubilant mood, as Freia, who tends the Golden Apples of Immortality (XVII STAR), has been successfully ransomed from the giants and returned safely to them.

Pages in Tarot indicate youthful energy, beginnings, and announcements. PAGE THOR here acts dynamically in accordance with the energetic element of his fire suit. He dramatically officiates the opening of Valhalla for the gods; Wagner's stately music, *Entrance of the Gods into Valhalla* accompanies the gods as they proceed across THOR'S Rainbow Bridge, eager to take up life in their exclusive new castle.

Divinatory Meaning

A storm is about to clear, and you will soon discover an unexpected opening, either physically or energetically. What previously appeared as a dead end, now opens up before you. A path to a desired goal, opportunity, or new vista that has been hidden or obstructed is about to be revealed: pay attention!

You may be moving to a higher level of comprehension in your life by understanding your "soul mission," for according to esotericism, we can each individually build a rainbow bridge in mental matter that connects us inwardly to the wisdom of our soul.

This card offers powerful protection as you proceed forward.

Reversed: If PAGE THOR is reversed, heed the Storm Warnings! There will be a temporary block or obstruction. Lay low until the weather changes and clears.

Divinatory Meanings of the 78 Cards

Page of Walsungs

YOUNG SIEGFRIED

(Siegfried)

Card Background

A reflective SIEGFRIED, here the unhappy orphan who lives isolated in the forest with his supposed father Mime the dwarf, contemplates his own reflection in a woodland pool. He is trying to understand how he can look so completely different from Mime, who claims to be his biological father. SIEGFRIED as Water PAGE is attempting to solve the deep mystery of his own origins. Suspecting he has been raised only on lies, PAGE SIEGFRIED intuits the truth that Mime is really no genetic relation to him at all. What he discovers here in his own reflection fuels his resolve to pry the truth from the dissembling Mime.

Divinatory Meaning

This is the Page of the emotional plane and of personal feeling. The card suggests that we are engaged in an effort similar to that of PAGE SIEGFRIED in figuring out a perplexing circumstance or trying to come to grips with an unresolved situation in our life. Careful observation of and reflection on the facts will aid us in finding answers.

The solace of Nature can be a powerful healing balm, allowing us to think things through in quiet, creative contemplation. Perhaps in a solitary "soul search" we find an important clue and an answer may be revealed as well. Whatever we discover empowers us to take decisive action in the matter at hand.

Reversed: A PAGE of WALSUNGS reversed indicates that the solution to a family problem or dilemma will remain elusive for now. Becoming totally self-absorbed in a private or personal matter will not help. For now, let go of the need to find all the answers. Adopt a different strategy to lessen self-obsession by engaging socially with others.

Divinatory Meanings of the 78 Cards

Page of Gibichungs
INNOCENT **SIEGFRIED**

(Twilight of The Gods)

Card Background

This card depicts SIEGFRIED immediately after unwittingly drinking Hagen's "Magic Potion of Forgetting," offered to him by Gutrune (QUEEN of NIBELUNGS). Having just lost all memory of his most holy consort Brunnhilde (V HIEROPHANT), he is alone and vulnerable in the enemy camp. He has forgotten what he most needs to remember!

Divinatory Meaning

PAGE SIEGFRIED puts you on notice that your inexperience or lack of mental discernment in a matter may cause you to miscalculate or make a serious mistake. All may not be as it appears on the surface. You may be trusting self-serving people who only want to use you for their own hidden agendas. It would be wise to do a background check on those you have just met, before accepting any offers or entering into any agreements. Be on your guard and proceed carefully.

PAGE SIEGFRIED is a card of counsel to conduct research and to acquire more information and to vet a situation before jumping to conclusions. Do not act impulsively in the current situation.

Drawing this Page of the mental plane also indicates that it is imperative to clearly remember something important from the past. What is it?

Reversed: A reversed SWORD PAGE SIEGFRIED advises that in this instance you need not be bound by the past. Let go of any old memories that may be holding you back.

Divinatory Meanings of the 78 Cards

Page of Nibelungs

SIEGFRIED

AT MIME'S FORGE

(Siegfried)

Card Background

Young SIEGFRIED works here at Mime's forge to repair the broken sword of his dead father Siegmund. Mime, his dwarf guardian, had preserved the sword fragments acquired from his pregnant mother Sieglinde when she found refuge years earlier, just prior to dying in childbirth, inside Mime's forge. Mime had kept the broken sword secret until SIEGFRIED demanded the truth of his birth.

In the card, PAGE SIEGFRIED has just discovered this great legacy. Overjoyed at his new inheritance, he has impatiently snatched the broken metal pieces away from Mime (KNIGHT of NIBELUNGS), who is engaged in yet another futile attempt to repair the sword, and begins reforging it himself. Though he is no metal smith and has no technical training or acquired skill, PAGE SIEGFRIED succeeds where the master Mime could not, fulfilling Wanderer Wotan's (IX HERMIT) prediction that only "one who knows no fear" could make the sword whole again.

Divinatory Meaning

Similar to Mime as KNIGHT OF NIBELUNGS, this is also a card of the will to form and create on the physical plane. Youthful NIBELUNG PAGE SIEGFRIED represents "beginner's mind," however, in contrast to the experience and technical mastery of the metalsmithing KNIGHT MIME. This card indicates that you are able to succeed at something through sheer creative élan in the inspiration of the moment, rather than through acquired training or expertise. You meet with unexpected success, grace, and achievement in an initial and wholly inspired effort.

Take advantage of this timely opportunity offered here, because it is an unusually fortunate and singular circumstance, which may not be repeated any time soon. This is also a card of claiming a birthright, or of inheriting something personally valuable from the past.

By divine grace or magical inspiration you successfully put all the pieces together! Congratulations!

Reversed: A reversed NIBELUNG PAGE SIEGFRIED suggests that the time is not quite right, and any forming attempts may be frustrated and unsuccessful. Not all energies are currently in right alignment, so the various pieces of a creation, project, or plan do not fall together and meld. Step back, reformulate, and make another attempt again later.

The FOUR Landscape Aces

> "The Aces…are quite above,
> and distinct from the other small cards…"
>
> —Aleister Crowley
> *Book of Thoth*

Before I had read these two quotes, I purposely wanted *The Ring Cycle Tarot* Aces to be easily distinguishable and to stand alone from the trumps, courts, and pips of this deck. So while I designed them to set a definite mood for their respective suits, I was apparently acting at the time from a deeper intuition than I consciously knew.

In Tarot, although Aces are numbered "1," the usual interpretation is Aces "high"—as each embodies the pure potential, motive force, and full power of its unique element. Upright Aces, as the tools of the Magician, are auspicious, and signify available "charged" energies that initiate new opportunities.

> "Ultimately, there are not 56 cards in the Minor Arcana of the Tarot. There are only 4—*the four aces*. The other 52 small cards…live inside the 4 aces."
>
> —L.M. DuQuette
> *Understanding Aleister Crowley's Thoth Tarot*

Ace of Gods

(The Valkyrie)

The Card: HEIGHTS OF VALHALLA

The lofty mountain heights in the background of this card are the exclusive abode of the gods, and the site of their palace Valhalla. No one else—neither demi-gods, giants, dwarves, nor living humans—has any right of access to it. All appears serene and inviolate. But the stars just beginning to appear in the gathering twilight foreshadow the darkness that will soon overtake this high place.

Divinatory Meaning

As the suit of Gods is the element of fire, this Ace has, as its highest meaning, our potential for communing with the Divine Spark of Spirit residing within each of us. This Ace suggests that now is the time to align with our highest aspirations and ideals, as they are necessary to the situation at hand. Further, we are currently in a mode of heightened energy and perspective. We have support for our worthy endeavors from unseen powers acting on our behalf. The sky is the limit!

Reversed: Our alignment to the highest within and without us fluctuates. Our inspiration proves unreliable. We need to climb to higher ground and gain a broader view.

Divinatory Meanings of the 78 Cards

Ace of Walsungs

(The Valkyrie)

The Card: A Forest Glade

The suit of WALSUNGS, the demi-gods of *The Ring Cycle*, corresponds to the plane of feeling and emotion. This Ace pictures a peaceful, secluded, and poetic forest clearing on an inspiring, warm autumn afternoon. The tree stump is an inviting place to sit, sort out feelings, and set goals and intentions. The craggy background mountains, the uneven ground, and a gathering wind, however, suggest the trials and even severe difficulties to which all the Walsungs, in spite of their beauty and great heart, are subjected.

Divinatory Meaning

Great potential for emotional fulfillment is realized, if you can meet new challenges and successfully pass unexpected tests of character. This Ace always bids you to lead with your heart, generosity of spirit, and inclusivity—as they will prove your best allies and protection in uncertain circumstances. This *Ring Cycle Tarot* Ace indicates that you now feel ready to explore fascinating but perhaps unfamiliar and even problematic territory. If you set out on an adventure, all goes well if you maintain sharp senses and a buoyant attitude. Convey your gratitude to Nature.

Reversed: You do not feel quite equal to a challenging opportunity being offered and decide to play it safe by staying with the known and familiar. Carefully examine the motive for your choice here: is this decision based on heeding a warning "gut feeling"—or instead, on a lack of confidence in yourself and a loss of nerve?

Ace of Gibichungs

(Twilight of The Gods)

The Card: WINTER SNOWSTORM

A powerful storm has formed on the mental plane. This card illustrates a freezing winter landscape beneath a threatening and turbulent sky. It suggests the dark and dangerous Gibichung kingdom of frozen, unredeemed feelings, including cold calculation, murderous betrayal, and revenge.

This image also reflects Wotan's isolated state of mind in the final music drama: stricken with grief, loneliness, and remorse over having banished Brunnhilde and, then more recently, having had his ruling spear shattered by his upstart grandson Siegfried, who did not know him. Wotan has withdrawn from actively participating in his own world. Now, as the desolation of this image conveys, he leaves fate to others—a fate that includes the duplicitous Gibichung humans, tragically manipulated by Alberich's son Hagen.

Divinatory Meanings of the 78 Cards

Divinatory Meaning

Unspoken or unacknowledged ideas and feelings swirl in a highly charged mental atmosphere. It is possible that adversaries, pretending to be helpful to your interests, may be working against you. Yet yellow sunlight breaks through the dense cloud cover. The challenge of this *Ring Cycle* Ace is to keep your wits about you. Use your thoughts inspirationally to penetrate the dense, oppressive atmosphere of negativity and defeat. By creatively employing the positive power of your own ideas, you can disperse any mental bad weather and turmoil that may be swirling around you.

Reversed: The dense clouds break up and evaporate, as the air clears with regard to your thinking. A storm passes over you and a spring thaw is at work beneath all the immobilizing mental ice and snow. Clarity is suddenly possible. All involved welcome an opportunity to "come clean" and deal openly and transparently.

The Card: EARTH CHASM

Deep in an ancient forest, the dragon Fafner prowls before an inaccessible and forbidding, steep, craggy cleft in the earth. He guards a nearby cave containing all his Nibelung treasure, which includes the IV TARNHELM and XV RING of POWER. This ACE of the physical and material plane reminds us that it is all too easy to become overly attached and obsessive like a hoarding dragon about desiring material riches, accumulating possessions, social status, and "success" as others define it.

Divinatory Meaning

There is great wealth hidden in a secret place. Of what might this wealth consist? How will you discover its location? What plan is needed to uncover and retrieve it? Do you have the necessary strength, integrity, and strategy to overcome the power that fiercely protects it?

Reversed: Something of material importance to you remains veiled, hidden, misplaced, or lost. While you may currently feel defeated, bide your time, and watch carefully for the next opening or opportunity. Then act decisively.

Ace of Nibelungs

(The Valkyrie, Siegfried)

Pips/Number/Small Cards

Suit of Gods
FIRE-WANDS

ELEMENT FIRE

At the top of *The Ring's* food chain, the race of Gods corresponds to the traditional Tarot suit of WANDS. Inspiration, will and passion, grand designs, and swift action are their hallmark. In divination, the Gods rule all these with fiery force.

2 of Gods

(Siegfried)

THE CARD: **Wotan's Ravens**

In a fierce snowstorm Wotan's two ravens, HUGIN (Thought) and MUGIN (Memory), fly over the world each day, reporting back to him in Valhalla what they observe in the world—especially concerning the fate of Siegfried and the Ring of Power.

Divinatory Meaning

This is a card of exploration, scouting, fact-finding—perhaps even of covert reconnaissance. These two ravens gather information by unique means, devising an overview that employs strategic detachment. This card advises you to see the big picture and take the broad view.

The 2 of GODS may also indicate a compatible partnership in which two fly together successfully navigating the storm.

Reversed: You do not have enough pertinent information; more research is needed. Do not give away your power to others. A partnership undergoes a change.

Divinatory Meanings of the 78 Cards

3 of Gods

(The Valkyrie)

Divinatory Meaning

You wrestle with a difficult decision. This card suggests taking a "time out" to think things through alone, as you are experiencing the horns of a dilemma and every course of action is problematic.

Summon your resourcefulness. You may decide to circumvent a shortsighted authority, or resist orders that do not make sense. Even if you make a moral choice for the highest good in the longest run as you see it, be prepared to pay the price and defend your actions. While there may be no way around difficulty in the current situation, avoid becoming entirely engulfed in drama. "To thine own self be true" and "Virtue is its own reward" underscore the meaning of this card.

The Card: **Brunnhilde in The Wild**

Brunnhilde wrestles with her thoughts in the solitude of nature, in despair over Wotan's revised orders demanding that Siegmund now be killed instead of saved in the upcoming battle with Hunding. How can she even entertain the idea of disobeying her father's new orders? And yet, at the same time, how can she possibly act against what she knows to be Wotan's own true will in the situation—which is surely to save his beloved son Siegmund's life?

Reversed: You may be acting without adequate thought, perhaps blindly obeying orders that, on reflection, will prove misguided for all concerned. Or you waffle in indecision. This reverse may also mean a release from a dilemma based on new information you are about to receive.

4 of Gods

(The Rhinegold)

The Card: Cavorting Rhinemaidens

In the very beginning of *The Ring Cycle*, the three Rhinemaidens joyfully swim and dive in their river waters, secure in the light of the scintillating Rhinegold. For the moment all is bliss, as they revel freely in an unrestrained expression of high spirits and natural grace. At this point in the epic, similar to the gods, the Rhinemaidens feel completely inviolable.

Divinatory Meaning

Let the Good Times Roll! Celebrate! Celebrate! Dance to the Music! Let go and have a Good Time. Attend or throw a party! Afterwards you will be able to return to everyday mundane tasks with renewed enthusiasm and inspiration.

Reversed: Take your duty as a caretaker and guardian of something important seriously. Do not let down your guard or lose yourself in distractions and amusements. This is not the time for rest or celebration—maintain disciplined focus on your appointed task. Be diligent and keep on keeping on.

Divinatory Meanings of the 78 Cards

5 of Gods

(The Rhinegold)

The Card: Fading Immortality

Five gods wither, sicken, and age as the giants Fasolt and Fafner in payment for building Valhalla have taken Freia, who tends the Golden Apples of Immortality, hostage. Wotan had agreed to this—never intending to pay up. But the bill has finally come due, and without Freia's Apples all the gods, including Wotan himself, begin to fade and age.

Divinatory Meaning

The esoteric name for this card is "Lord of Strife," here describing a high-pressure situation and a desperate state of affairs. You are in dire need of the sustenance the Golden Apples provide—what do they symbolize in your life? Time is fast running out! Quickly formulate and implement a plan of action.

A group argument may erupt between disagreeing factions.

Reversed: In a crisis, you formulate a creative solution that defuses the pressure. There is a reinstatement of stability. You find an ingenious way to stop the clock, reset the hourglass, and save the day!

6 of Gods

(The Valkyrie)

THE CARD: **Wotan Exiles Brunnhilde**

Hail to Wotan, the Conquering Hero and King of the Gods, who has maintained the rule of law, and brooked no disobedience from his rebellious daughter Brunnhilde! After stripping her of immortality and Valkyrie status, Wotan has just put her to sleep, having ordered Loge to kindle the protective Ring of Magic Fire, the source of light in this card. The fire will imprison her until a future hero claims her for his bride.

Divinatory Meaning

This is the card of being "Master and Commander," "Top Dog," and "Calling All the Shots." You maintain leadership, setting all the rules and terms for others. You are the triumphant victor, the acknowledged and respected "King of the Hill."

But this includes taking full responsibility for your choices and decisions. Be fair and just in your position of authority, for, as exemplified by Wotan, bad decisions and abuse of power will surely come back to haunt you.

Reversed: Your current victory may prove Pyrrhic. You experience a sorrowful farewell with its attendant heartbreak and grief. A decision could go against you.

Divinatory Meanings of the 78 Cards

7 of Gods

7 of Gods

(The Rhinegold)

The Card: Freia Is Taken Hostage

The goddess Freia, who tends the Golden Apples of Immortality, is taken hostage by the giants Fasolt and Fafner, as agreed upon with Wotan, to pay for constructing Valhalla. Lacking Freia's Apples, the gods will now begin to age, sicken, and die if Wotan cannot quickly find a fortune with which to ransom her back.

Divinatory Meaning

You are being held hostage to an unsuitable situation, or to the small-minded thinking of others around you. There is overt opposition to your ideas, plans, and projects. You are stalemated. Serious obstacles must be overcome. Still it is important to maintain your courage and hold your position, even if you are captive to a difficult situation. Make an appeal for outside assistance, but at the same time raise your own efforts to a new level. Dig in and "grind it out" from behind the baseline, for this card counsels unwavering valor under duress.

Reversed: A solution from "out of the blue" redeems a difficult situation. You are free once again!

8 of Gods

(The Valkyrie)

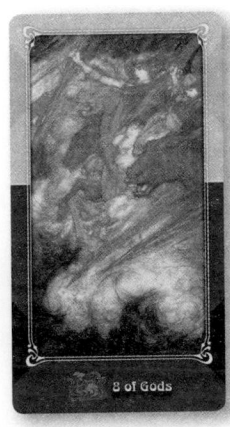

THE CARD: **The Ride of the Valkyries!**

Hoyotoho, Hoyotoho, Heiaha, Heiaha!

Eight of the Valkyries (the ninth, Brunnhilde, lags behind to save Sieglinde) race to their mountaintop meeting place, carrying with them heroic warriors who have just died in battle. They had agreed to assemble there before returning all together to Valhalla with their newly handpicked conscripts for the elite security guard that protects the gods there.

Wagner's musical accompaniment to this scene is by far the most recognizable and popular piece of music he ever wrote—nearly everyone, whether or not they have ever heard *The Ring Cycle*, can hum it on cue. It was used in the film *Apocalypse Now* and as a cartoon staple.

1.
Divinatory Meanings of the 78 Cards

Divinatory Meaning

The High-Energy card of this deck! It denotes flying on the wings of Inspiration at great speed. All the forces of the Valkyries' lightning spears, and those of their supernatural horses, are in unified alignment. Everything is directed with a single purpose towards a single goal. The Valkyries lend an intense focus to the task at hand.

United in group solidarity, they move forward together with great excitement and vitality. Yet there is also implied grounding in the physical plane, as the Valkyries depicted here, race down toward earth.

This card, to whatever it may pertain in a spread, represents the thrilling, unleashed enthusiasm and energy of high tide. Not much can stop the Valkyries at full gallop! Throw yourself into whole-hearted action and Go For It!

Reversed: You have lost sight of your goal. Energy is dissipated, misdirected, at cross-purposes, and it eddies in interference patterns. There is general confusion rather than clarity. Collective endeavors fall apart. You go in circles. Stop, rethink, and regroup.

9 of Gods

(The Rhinegold)

The Card: Loge the Trickster

Fire elemental Loge is deep beneath the earth in Alberich's cavernous Nibelhome, engaged in an attempt to steal the dwarf's fabulous treasure hoard. He and Wotan need it to ransom the goddess Freia back from the giants, who have taken her captive in payment for building Valhalla. In the card, Loge engages in the pretense of being terrified by Alberich, (who has just used the TARNHELM XIV ART to shape-shift into a huge serpent) in an attempt to put the dwarf off his guard by feeding his egotism. Contrary to appearances, Loge here is really in a position of strength.

Divinatory Meaning

Stand your ground and fend off an attack. Consider engaging in a playful defensive strategy of pretense to throw your opposition off guard. By disguising your true motives from a threatening adversary, you succeed in your objective. To master the situation, try using a clever theatrical ploy in lieu of physical strength.

Reversed: It is time to beat a hasty retreat, as you risk being overwhelmed and defeated by greater forces. At this point, your own strategy is inadequate and will, in all likelihood, fail.

Divinatory Meanings of the 78 Cards

10 of Gods

(The Rhinegold)

THE CARD: **The Giants Examine Freia's Ransom**

Fasolt and Fafner examine the Nibelung Treasure Hoard—all stolen from loveless Alberich the dwarf by Wotan and Loge. It is offered to the giants in exchange for the Goddess Freia, who was the originally agreed-upon price for building Valhalla. Fasolt points out that he can still see the gleam of Freia's eye through a hole in the treasure pile. Fafner will demand the Ring of Power, now on Wotan's hand, to cover it up. Wotan, however, will refuse to relinquish the Ring.

Freia can only await the outcome of their negotiations. Without her Golden Apples of Immortality, the gods will sicken, age, and will soon die.

Divinatory Meaning

This card describes a very uncomfortable and disagreeable state of affairs; a traditional designation here is "Oppression." Prisoner to a difficult situation, you are at the mercy of unreasoning or blind forces beyond your control. You find yourself in a high stakes holding pattern, and there is not much you can do except to wait patiently for the next turn of events. Momentarily you feel a victim of unfortunate circumstances, but an offer made on your behalf by others is being critically examined and carefully negotiated. Remain calm and brave.

You could also, however, be partly restricted in this binding situation by your own limited ideas and by an outdated habitual way of thinking or doing things. An internal change of attitude might help hasten your release.

Reversed: Too much emphasis has been placed on the material side of life, and you feel its restrictive weight. Negotiations in which you have an important stake, but no direct voice, come to a standstill. Forbearance is required on your part.

Pips/Number/Small Cards

Suit of Walsungs
WATER-CUPS

A race of demi-gods engendered by Wotan, King of the Gods, and an (un-named) human woman, corresponding to the suit of CUPS and the element of water. Walsungs rule love, emotions, feelings and desire, along with the realm of the family.

ELEMENT WATER

2 of Walsungs

(Twilight of The Gods)

Brunnhilde, having long been banished from Valhalla by her father Wotan and stripped of her godhood and Valkyrie status, now gives her whole commitment to the Walsung. Here she and Siegfried affirm their enduring holy love for one another.

Divinatory Meaning

In *The Ring Cycle* deck, this is one of the highest cards for purely romantic love and a shared commitment. It depicts the dynamic optimal combination of male and female energies—which can apply to two people, or alternately, to the animus and anima within each individual psyche. This card expresses the synergistic fire created by a partnership of two acknowledged "kindred spirits." The message of this card is to openly acknowledge what is truly in our hearts.

Reversed: Be prepared for romantic tests and challenges ahead. This could mean a short-lived love affair or an unrequited love. You may be unwittingly or unrealistically projecting your own desires, needs, and feelings onto someone else. Test the emotional waters before diving into them headfirst.

The Card: The Embrace

SIEGFRIED the WALSUNG has braved the Ring of Fire that protected Brunnhilde for twenty years, and he has awakened her from her long sleep with a kiss. The two declare their mutual recognition and love for one another in an ecstatic embrace. They pledge to set one another ablaze in passion.

Divinatory Meanings of the 78 Cards

3 of Walsungs

3 of Walsungs

(The Valkyrie)

The Card: In Hunding's Hut

Hunding sits at the head of his table attended by his wife Sieglinde. He has reluctantly offered the mysterious stranger the hospitality of his hut for the night, only because it is the law of the land. What could be an enjoyable social occasion, however, is marred by complex dark unspoken undercurrents. One of these is Siegmund's dawning ironic realization that Hunding is the very enemy from whom he has just fled and from whom he thought he had safely escaped!

Divinatory Meaning

You now put together the pieces of a puzzling situation to discern the truth. You find a short-lived reprieve from danger; but there could be enemies in your camp, so tread and speak carefully. This card can connote a business partnership or cooperative effort in which there may be a three-way power struggle. There is the possibility of a love triangle.

Reversed: It is time to plan some recreation with good friends. Seek enjoyment and safety in their company, or at a community/collective event. Reaching an equitable agreement with others is now possible.

4 of Walsungs
(The Valkyrie)

The Card: **Brunnhilde and Grane**

Above the River Rhine, the water in this card, Brunnhilde is confident of Wotan's initial orders that she is to protect Siegmund the Walsung in his upcoming combat with Hunding. She enjoys a momentary calm from the heights in the company of her beloved magical steed VII CHARIOT—GRANE. While awaiting the end of Fricka's "words" with Wotan, she empathetically tunes into Nature.

Divinatory Meaning

Good luck and well-being on all levels are yours for the moment. Take a short, deserved, refreshing break in the respite and beauty of nature, communing with the plant and animal kingdoms. You have chosen the high road well. The traditional designation for this card—"Blended Pleasure"—is conveyed through the devoted companionship of Brunnhilde the Valkyrie and Grane, her magical equine mount. But be careful—pride goes before a fall.

Reversed: There is a dramatic turn of events. Expect a change of orders.

Divinatory Meanings of the 78 Cards

5 of Walsungs

(Siegfried)

The Card: Sieglinde Lost in the Snow

Sieglinde, having been saved from Wotan's death decree by a rebellious Brunnhilde acting against his orders, is now alone, lost in a vast forest. Her twin and lover, Siegmund, has just been killed in battle by Hunding. Her savior Brunnhilde is now banished and imprisoned. Pregnant with their son Siegfried, she struggles to find shelter from the snowstorm.

Divinatory Meaning

You may be finding yourself, similar to Sieglinde, feeling lost, disoriented, and in need of support. You are experiencing trying and difficult events, perhaps even a great personal sorrow. The only way to surmount the present challenges is to summon self-reliance and perseverance. If you weather this storm bravely and keep moving forward, you will find assistance ahead. Follow the light.

Reversed: If reversed, expect unexpected release from a seemingly hopeless situation.

6 of Walsungs
(Siegfried)

THE CARD: **Orphan Siegfried Observes a Wolf Family**

As a child still in Mime's charge, Siegfried wistfully observes a nurturing wolf family in the wild at twilight, noticing how they all resemble one another. The lack of these qualities in his own life causes Siegfried to doubt Mime's professed paternity.

Divinatory Meaning

There is a longing for emotional fulfillment in different circumstances. Alone, you experience a nostalgia for happy times past or yet to be. You may feel like an orphan, seeking the warmth and support of a close family or social unit.

Seemingly accidental information or careful observation of the natural world may lead you to new conclusions. Pay close attention to a synchronicity that may prove illuminating, and signal a recovery from disappointment.

Reversed: You remain in the dark with respect to your unanswered questions. Your doubts, perhaps relating to paternity, continue to persist. You feel exiled from your true home.

Divinatory Meanings of the 78 Cards

7 of Walsungs

(Siegfried)

Divinatory Meaning

A confrontation with either an external or internal dragon is at hand. This dragon represents a primal force or a situation you must face with courage. You must step out of your usual comfort zone and be willing to fight for yourself, your beliefs, and convictions: make a bold choice that results in bold action.

With a definite plan in mind, you prove equal to a difficult or dangerous confrontation. You identify, engage, and overcome your fears, "slaying" obstructing illusions and conditioned or acculturated beliefs that stand in your way.

The Card: Siegfried Engages Fafner

Siegfried has accepted Mime's challenge to slay the dragon Fafner—and to thereby perhaps learn fear. Siegfried, caring nothing for the treasure, but only wanting to prove himself, attacks Fafner with his reforged sword Nothung in hand, after Fafner categorically states his intention to eat him!

Reversed: In the face of an external threat, the odds are against you, so don't be lured into a battle you cannot win. Stand your ground, but do not become the aggressor. Use your wits and try talking your way around or out of a challenge. If this fails, back off—as you have neither the energy nor the strategy needed to win at this point.

8 of Walsungs

(Twilight of The Gods)

THE CARD: **Brunnhilde and Waltraute**

The Valkyrie Waltraute has sought out her sister Brunnhilde in exile on her fire-ringed rock plateau and pleads with her to return the Ring of Power to the Rhinemaidens, so that the gods may (as she believes) be saved. Brunnhilde, however, having been stripped of her godly and Valkyrie status years previously by Wotan, now considers herself a Walsung, by virtue of her "marriage" to Siegfried. As the Ring of Power is his cherished love token to her and the seal of their union, Brunnhilde refuses to give it up.

Divinatory Meanings of the 78 Cards

Divinatory Meaning

In *The Ring Cycle Tarot* this is a card of a confrontation, with no resolution probable at the present time. One of the parties involved may well adopt a "hold-out" attitude. If that is you, your refusal results from steadfastly and rightly defending your own beliefs and values when offered an unsatisfying arrangement or deal. Your search for the higher good, as you understand it, means you may have to go your own way alone if necessary. This is not the time to compromise where deeply held beliefs and feelings are at issue.

Conversely, if you identify with Waltraute, the agent of appeal, your reasoned argument fails to win the day, as you find yourself up against an immovable emotional force.

In questions regarding health, this card could signify an extremely dire prognosis, as Valkyries are the harbingers of death. A "live or die" choice has to be made. The good news is that if the party involved maintains an unflinching will and resolve in the face of such a serious threat, a complete recovery can be made. But whatever the ultimate choice, it needs to be respected.

Reversed: You may have buckled under to external pressure, acting only from expediency. If you signed on to a cause in which you do not really believe just to keep the peace with others, you are selling yourself seriously short.

The Card: Siegfried Finds Brunnhilde

Guided by the Woodbird, Siegfried has scaled the mountain summit and passed through the Ring of Fire. Here he catches his first glimpse of the sleeping Brunnhilde. At this moment, he is on top of the world, undefeated, sure of his prowess, and fully confident in his great personal destiny.

9 of Walsungs

(Siegfried)

Divinatory Meaning

You are at the top of your game! As you have mastered difficulties and passed the tests, all good things come to you now. You are on the brink of an unexpected, exciting discovery. There is a possible meeting with a kindred spirit or soulmate. Lon DuQuette denotes the 9 of Cups, "One of the best cards in the deck."

Reversed: You have climbed to the top of the mountain, but what you sought is not there. Perhaps you have been following a false trail? Check your position: you may need to retrace your steps.

Divinatory Meanings of the 78 Cards

10 of Walsungs

10 of Walsungs

(Siegfried)

The Card: **The Love Call**

High Noon in Overachievers' Heaven: Siegfried, a heroic Walsung demi-god, and Brunnhilde, the former "Miss Valkyrie World," proclaim their mutual love for one another in an ecstatic moment. For the first time both discover a loving companion and "kindred spirit." We see the couple on a great height, both physically and emotionally, in which the once-restrictive Ring of Fire is now transformed into leaping flames of passion and desire.

Divinatory Meaning

Truly this is a card of "Perfected Happiness." You experience peak emotional satisfaction. You have successfully completed a trial by fire, and you now enjoy well-earned high self-esteem. This card celebrates a meeting of the minds and hearts, and may suggest the possibility of a romantic liaison, an engagement, or a marriage.

Reversed: This is a card of delayed gratification. "The course of True Love never did run straight." Your emotional expectations, possibly including a romantic partnership, remain unfulfilled for the present. But all is certainly not lost—more time is needed to solidify deeply experienced mutual feelings.

Pips/Number/Small Cards

Suit of Gibichungs
AIR-SWORDS

ELEMENT AIR

In divination, the Gibichungs rule the power of all ideas and thinking—both negative and positive—along with the entire mental body that includes both concrete and abstract thought.

Divinatory Meanings of the 78 Cards

2 of Gibichungs

(Twilight of The Gods)

further reveals that she left Siegfried's back unprotected, knowing he would choose to face any challenge head on. Hagen thus learns of Siegfried's hidden vulnerability to mortal attack.

Divinatory Meaning

Balance is needed in the current situation. Strive to be fair. Because you may not have all the facts, the necessary information, or the true story, do not jump to conclusions, act in haste, or reveal secrets—all of which you may regret. Revenge is a low emotion and an unworthy motivation for action, as it will only perpetuate more tragedy.

At the same time, be on your guard for plots and counterplots in which others may be trying to involve and manipulate you.

The Card: A Plot of Betrayal

Brunnhilde, convinced she has been cruelly and deliberately deceived by Siegfried, who has just married Gutrune—but not knowing the true circumstances—plots her revenge with Hagen. She tells him that she provided a magical, protective, energetic shield for Siegfried that deflects all weaponry. Then, in an uncharacteristic fit of fury, she

Reversed: It is now crucial to make your position and your side of the story known to all others concerned in the current situation. Do not withhold what you know; otherwise, serious misunderstandings may lead to an unfortunate turn of events.

3 of Gibichungs

(Twilight of The Gods)

THE CARD: The Fatal Hunt

Hagen, acting in revenge for his father Alberich, plunges his spear into Siegfried's back—the only place the hero is vulnerable to attack. The guise of a hunt is being used as a cover for this premeditated murder. Siegfried is betrayed for his Ring of Power and becomes the third victim of the Curse of the Ring. Wotan's ravens circle above, bearing witness to the killing.

Divinatory Meanings of the 78 Cards

Divinatory Meaning

This is a card of deep grief and sorrow caused here by betrayal and revenge. The sin of the father (Wotan's theft of Alberich's Ring) is visited on the unknowing grandson Siegfried. Notice how Hunding's spear penetrates Siegfried's heart chakra from the back. Could someone you trust be undermining or plotting against you? This card carries the warning to watch your back lest you come to grief.

Still, a sacrifice may need to be made facing Karma from the past that results in pain, suffering, and loss.

Carl Gustav Jung (1875-1961), Swiss psychotherapist/psychiatrist, was a progenitor of the unconscious and transcendent functions of the psyche. In Jung's view, Siegfried represents that part of our true self we all must tragically sacrifice in the adaptation necessary to participate in our larger collective society.

In a positive view, this card can indicate the sudden death of a life situation no longer serving the highest good, crucial to continued growth.

Reversed: You are granted an eleventh-hour reprieve. A plot against you is discovered in the nick of time. Give thanks and gratitude! You escape a dire attack!

4 of Gibichungs

(The Rhinegold)

dissolved when Alberich realizes the Rhinemaidens are only teasing him and laughing at his crude amorous efforts. The unintended consequences of their seemingly harmless but insensitive flirtation at his expense will prove world shattering.

Divinatory Meaning

This is a battle of wills and opposing viewpoints. For the moment, a balance of forces and equilibrium is achieved. However, this fragile stability may prove short-lived and can presage great change. Underestimating an opponent, failure to correctly read a situation, or engaging in an unthinking seemingly harmless prank could prove explosive.

Someone's previously contained unbridled egotism could now become a threat.

The Card: Unstable Equilibrium

This is the depiction, early on in the first music drama, of an unstable equilibrium between Alberich and the three Rhinemaidens. Alberich grabs onto a Rhinemaiden with the intent of securing romantic love, but she resists him with equal strength. Soon the truce will be

Reversed: There is a continuing uneasy truce and balance of opposite energies. A situation remains unchanged for good or ill—expect more of the same. Stasis.

Divinatory Meanings of the 78 Cards

5 of Gibichungs

(The Rhinegold)

Divinatory Meaning

This is a card of winning or losing a mental engagement, and of the endless alternation of light and dark, both in the psyche and in the world. It can be the ongoing struggle in the mind between things as we might want them to be and how they actually are. This is the "winner take all" paradigm—which cannot be sustained in the long run.

Something of importance is being contested, and there is much at stake. Stay on the alert as rightful ownership or position may be threatened. Find a way to beat the odds against you.

The dwarf Alberich represents our deep emotional wounds, which can prove destructive to the world if we act out from them. The Rhinemaidens in turn here exemplify how lack of compassion, callousness, and insensitivity to the suffering of others has its negative consequences as well.

The Card: Imminent Theft

Having just renounced all love forever, Alberich climbs up to steal the pure Rhinegold. The disbelieving Rhinemaidens have not yet taken this unimaginable decision seriously and still cast patronizing looks down at him. The fateful die has been cast, however, and the Rhinemaidens are about to face defeat and will soon be thrown into darkness.

Reversed: Make a decision to "go for the gold" regardless of the outcome. Initiate a bold, decisive, and radical move. A "win-win" situation is achieved by sharing a valuable resource or prize.

6 of Gibichungs

(The Rhinegold)

stolen their Rhinegold! Once he forges it into the Ring of Power, he will become Master of the World, amass a limitless fortune, and with it enslave them all! They urgently petition Loge's help for the return of their Gold. But as someone who will aid them in their just cause, he proves to be less than the best choice.

Divinatory Meaning

This is a card of petition for a fair reinstatement of something that has been taken from you. Because the Gibichung suit is that of the mental plane, this could be an idea, the power of your mind itself, or a creative formula or work that has been stolen and used by another. It is a plea for a fair hearing and for justice.

Reversed: If you make an appeal for justice, be certain to whom you are speaking; others may have their own personal agendas, of which you may be ignorant. Instead of being swamped by the high emotion of the moment, think things through. Important information could be conveyed to you at or near water.

The Card: The Rhinemaidens Report Theft of the Rhinegold

The three Rhinemaidens report to Loge that the unthinkable has happened—the dwarf Alberich has foresworn all love forever and

Divinatory Meanings of the 78 Cards

7 of Gibichungs

(The Rhinegold)

Fasolt claims the Ring for himself, Fafner immediately attacks and kills him for it. Alberich had just put a curse on the Ring proclaiming that whoever possesses it will be killed by another who covets it. All the gods bear horrified witness to this immediate first fulfillment of the Curse. The image graphically describes the fatal destiny awaiting all who wear the Ring of Power.

Divinatory Meaning

This is the card of Anger Management. You are engaged in a hostile confrontation, conflict or declaration of war, most probably one of opposing ideas, as this is a card of the mental plane. This could be an internal conflict of opposing inclinations or impulses, or possibly a "death battle" signaling a permanent rift between siblings, partners, or friends. Step back and defuse the anger, rather than impulsively acting on it. The best course of action is to simply walk away from an explosive situation and allow time and space to calm your mind.

Reversed: Reconciliation prevails, as partners find a way to resolve their conflict.

The Card: **Alberich's Curse**

Fasolt and Fafner, the two giant brothers, engage in a murderous fight over ownership of the Ring of Power. It was part of the Nibelung treasure hoard that Wotan stole from the dwarf Alberich to pay (in lieu of the goddess Freia) for the construction of Valhalla. When

8 of Gibichungs

(Siegfried)

The Card: Self-Enslaving Thoughts

ALBERICH, completely consumed by longstanding hatred and revenge, keeps his vigil outside Fafner's cave, hoping somehow, in spite of this fierce dragon, to find a way to regain the Ring of Power. His every thought and action is tied to this single agenda. Since Wotan took the Ring from him by force, he feels entirely justified in his obsessive mindset.

Similar to Wotan, ALBERICH has engendered a son (HAGEN, KING OF GIBICHUNGS) for the sole purpose of helping him regain the Ring. Alberich sits here in the gloomy forest outside the dragon cave wasting his life by endlessly nursing his grievances and plotting his revenge.

Divinatory Meanings of the 78 Cards

Divinatory Meaning

Free yourself now from your entangling negative emotions and perceived past injustices. These old, injurious mental tapes of real or imagined grievances hold you back and interfere with your true potential. Disempower your obsessive thoughts of all kinds—physical, emotional, and, as this is a card of the mental plane, especially those of the mind. Step free of entangling thoughts and the habitually confining patterns they generate. Let go of the past and move on!

Alberich here exemplifies how wholly mentally corrosive the Ring of Power actually is. While it is difficult to extricate the mind from its all-engrossing obsessions, it can and must be done. Otherwise you will find yourself increasingly isolated, without friends, like delusional Alberich alone in a bleak landscape.

Reversed: You are currently engaged in your necessary "inner work" (perhaps therapy or spiritual practice) allowing you to free your mind. You are purifying your mental vehicle, your ideas, your emotions, your past. You are setting positive goals for yourself: what are they? All these ingredients and work preclude achieving the personal happiness you desire.

9 of Gibichungs

(Twilight of The Gods)

The Card: "Lord of Cruelty"

No one in the entire *Ring Cycle* fits the description of this card's esoteric name, "Lord of Cruelty and Despair," as well as ALBERICH. He has become a living nightmare, poisoned by toxic thinking. He begets a son, Hagen, for the sole purpose of infiltrating and manipulating the Gibichungs in a plot to recover the Ring of Power. Entirely consumed and obsessed by revenge and hate, ALBERICH learns absolutely nothing in the entire course of Wagner's epic. He lives in the past or in the future—but never in the present.

Divinatory Meaning

What past mental grievances or disappointments are you holding on to? Take this opportunity to examine them and then let them go. Detoxify your thinking! Any revenge or obsessive desires you continue to harbor will only disconnect you from others and your own Higher Self. Let go of painful memories and corrosive remorse, the "what ifs" and the "could have beens" in your internal life. Instead, identify your considerable gifts and talents. Change the mental scenery. Alberich is the negative warning example of what not to become: internally poisoned by mentally generated venom.

Reversed: Are you feeling manipulated? Or, are you manipulating others? Step out of "monkey mind" and lighten up! Now is the moment to release old grievances that are driving you—perhaps unconsciously.

Divinatory Meanings of the 78 Cards

10 of Gibichungs

(Twilight of The Gods)

the reclamation of their stolen Rhinegold! Here they prepare to drag Hagen to his death beneath the waters.

Divinatory Meaning

If you, like Hagen, have been consumed by a single selfish obsession, this card indicates a complete failure of plans and thwarted desire; MAYDAY! All is futility and you are about to be dragged down into the depths: LET GO! Loosen your grip. Immediately rethink and reformulate your goals and ambitions to be more inclusive.

If, like the Rhinemaidens, however, you have long sought restitution for an unfair or unjust situation, then this is a very good card indeed! Justice is finally done. Something of great value taken from you is returned. Here the Feminine Principle justly triumphs in the situation.

THE CARD: **The Rhinemaidens Triumphant**

After the final conflagration that destroys the gods' world has burnt itself out, Hagen, still desperately attempting to secure the Ring, has thrown himself into the overflowing Rhine waters in an effort to wrest it from the Rhinemaidens. They, however, will not be denied

Reversed: You experience a surprising and improbable success against long odds. Celebrate!

Pips/Number/Small Cards

Suit of Nibelungs
EARTH-DISKS, COINS, PENTACLES

ELEMENT EARTH

This suit corresponds to the suit of Disks/Coins/Pentacles. Living mostly underground, the dwarf Nibelungs command the elemental powers of the earth. They mine and forge all metals, especially loving gold. The "coin of the realm" is their domain. In divination, Nibelungs rule work and livelihood craftsmanship/artisanship and all things material.

Divinatory Meanings of the 78 Cards

2 of Nibelungs

(The Rhinegold)

Divinatory Meaning

This is a situation of unequal power, or at the least, of very difficult circumstances. You are enslaved in forced work, and/or others conscript your abilities and talents only for their own benefit. You may be working off a debt of material obligation.

In this card, Alberich may also represent your internal disciplinarian, who is reminding you there is a task you have ignored too long and that urgently needs your attention.

If you now have the power of command, be certain your goals (unlike Alberich's) invoke the highest good for yourself and all others concerned. The traditional Two of Disks alternation of energies is pictured in this card as the dramatic play of light and dark.

The Card: Alberich's Tyranny

The dwarf Alberich, who has renounced all love forever, stolen the Rhinegold, and forged the Ring of Power from it, here enslaves his brother Mime to do only his bidding. He is now forcing Mime to craft the magical (XIV MAGIC-TARNHELM) for him. Alberich has become a petty tyrant who uses his power only for selfish and base ends.

Reversed: You find release from a restrictive or difficult situation. You reclaim your freedom. Power is fairly shared.

3 of Nibelungs

(The Rhinegold)

Mime, Alberich, and the Tarnhelm complete the three active agents in this card, along with the three powers the Tarnhelm confers: invisibility, shape shifting, and instant transport. The esoteric name for this card, "Lord of Material Works" aptly describes Mime as the skilled creator of the magical Tarnhelm.

Divinatory Meaning

While this card shows Mime entirely disempowered and at the mercy of the invisible Alberich, it is instructing you to master your fear and, unlike Mime, claim your creative power! Learn from the misery of Mime's example and instead, stand up for yourself! Don't let others take credit for your ideas or your work.

Act on what you know to be true for yourself, especially with regard to your choice of work/vocation. Do not allow the agendas of others to derail you. Take pride in your creative gifts. Don't sell yourself short.

The Card: Fearful Craftsman Mime

While a card of three—all that appears visible in frame is the figure of Mime cowering in fear before Alberich, rendered invisible by the magic Tarnhelm. This is Mime's own magical creation, commissioned but then commandeered by his brother Alberich. Alberich turns Mime's own work against him, refusing him all credit for it.

Reversed: You are being undermined by the jealousy and envy of others for your gifts and talents. Additionally, it is now time to disempower any inner dysfunction of your own that may be negating your self worth.

Divinatory Meanings of the 78 Cards

4 of Nibelungs

(The Rhinegold)

now forge the stolen gold into the Ring of Power, claiming for himself, if only briefly, the status of "Lord of Earthly Power."

Divinatory Meaning

You are chasing something or someone of value that is currently proving elusive.

There could be a loss due to a breach in security or your failure to be vigilant.

You may be experiencing a situation in which you find another's motivations unexpected, surprising, and unfathomable.

Apply more focus and energy to your effort. Improve your speed—you need to be quicker off the mark mentally and/or physically. Try diving deeper and faster!

Reversed: You evade capture—in the short run—and escape with something valuable.

The Card: **The Rhinegold Is Stolen!**

Too late do the three Rhinemaidens spring into action in an attempt to stop Alberich—who has breached their defenses, renounced all love forever, and made off with their precious Rhinegold. Thinking they were inviolate, the Rhinemaidens were off their guard. The dwarf Alberich will

5 of Nibelungs

(Siegfried)

The Card: Opportunist Mime

This is the companion card to the 5 of Walsungs. The dense and hapless Mime, unappreciated as a master metal worker and abused by his brother Alberich, is out foraging in the snow. He is about to happen upon the lost and pregnant Sieglinde. More from a sense of some future gain than from any selfless generosity, Mime rescues Sieglinde and shelters her at his forge. When she dies in childbirth, he reluctantly raises her son Siegfried.

Divinatory Meaning

If you find yourself out in the cold, stay alert, as you may make a fortunate discovery. Hang on and pay attention. Your generosity towards others at this time will be well repaid. You could soon be assuming a nurturing or caretaking responsibility.

Reversed: Are you in a relationship from a sense of duty rather than of love? Is your resentment building from shouldering a heavy responsibility? While compassion and selflessness are good, you must balance these with your own needs, too. What have you overlooked? It's time to reevaluate your decisions.

Divinatory Meanings of the 78 Cards

6 of Nibelungs

(Siegfried)

his unused treasure does no one any good and only serves to isolate him from all interaction with the world at large.

Divinatory Meaning

If you identify with Fafner in this card, you now have the needed material resources to accomplish your goals—so use your resources creatively, instead of hoarding them. You may need to defend your realm from interlopers: don't shrink from your own strength.

If, however, you interpret dragon Fafner as your obstacle, play a waiting game, and look for a clear opening. A daring strategy is necessary to claim your treasure—don't act until you are fully prepared and confident you can meet the challenge.

Reversed: Are you being overprotective or downright paranoid? Dragon is a state of mind. Your best course of action now is to share your resources, including ideas, insights, and expertise. Break old habits by exploring and trying new things. Come out of your comfortable cave, meet new people, and engage with the world.

The Card: **Fafner Stands Guard**

The dragon Fafner, previously a giant who shape-shifted using the Tarnhelm, inhabits a cave deep in an ancient forest. There he vigilantly guards the Nibelung treasure, which includes the fateful and cursed Ring of Power. Although Fafner is now "Lord of Material Success,"

7 of Nibelungs

(Siegfried)

THE CARD: **Arguing Over Treasure**

The dwarf brothers Alberich and Mime, both equally bent on possessing the Ring, begin arguing over it. Having hidden in the wings while Siegfried did the real work of slaying the dragon Fafner (who had guarded the Nibelung treasure for nearly two generations), they now angrily confront one another over Fafner's body. (Siegfried has meanwhile returned to the cave to retrieve the Ring and Tarnhelm on instructions from the woodbird).

Although the treasure cave and all within it now belong to Siegfried by rights, Alberich and Mime are so obsessed with owning the Ring, they indulge in the fiction that it is now free for the taking. Both delude themselves into thinking it will be easy to eliminate Siegfried, whom they consider little more than a simple child.

This is the card of "Success Unfulfilled" and, for these two dwarves, the appellation fits perfectly, as neither one will ever again have possession of the Ring in the epic from this point on.

Divinatory Meanings of the 78 Cards

Divinatory Meaning

This is a card of the earth element and the material plane. There is ownership dispute over money, inheritance, real estate, a business, or intellectual property. A hotly contested argument can escalate into a lawsuit. While staking a claim and putting forth a position, be open to compromise and a shared settlement with all concerned parties. Otherwise be prepared for a lengthy ordeal (longer even than *The Ring Cycle*). This can also be a card of sibling rivalry.

Reversed: This card offers the possibility for resolution of a longstanding (family) disagreement and of coming to terms with a contentious past.

8 of Nibelungs

8 of Nibelungs

(Siegfried)

alone can reforge Siegmund's broken sword, Nothung? —which is the very question Mime, desperately needing the answer, should have asked of the Wanderer when he had the chance—but failed to! Unable to answer, Mime realizes he has lost his high stakes wager with the Wanderer—who he suddenly suspects is someone of much higher status than mere appearances indicate.

Divinatory Meaning

You are facing a challenge from an outside force. Do not act from overconfidence, impulse, or untested assumptions. Someone seemingly unlikely may have the pertinent information you require. *It is crucial to ask the right questions* as directly as possible, crafting your query carefully and thoughtfully.

The Card: Mime in The Wanderer's Shadow

Wotan in disguise as a wandering hermit (IX HERMIT) casts a dark, oblique shadow across the floor of dwarf Mime's forge. Mime and the Wanderer have been engaged in a contest of wits, each asking the other three questions. He who fails to answer a question correctly will forfeit his head to the other. Mime, having answered two of the Wanderer's questions correctly, is now stumped by his third: Who

Reversed: You see through another's disguise or false persona and are able to ascertain their true motives. You thus save yourself from a serious misstep. Freely admitting what you don't know gains you respect in the eyes of others.

Divinatory Meanings of the 78 Cards

9 of Nibelungs

(Siegfried)

The Card: No Free Lunch

Contrary to many traditional Nine of Disk cards, the only good fortune to be gained here is in trusting your gut instinct when sensing imminent danger! Mime offers food to his young charge, the orphan Siegfried. But while he pretends to be a caring and concerned parent, Mime has a sinister hidden agenda. He plans to nurture and then employ Siegfried's uncanny physical strength to slay the dragon Fafner who guards the Ring of Power. Then Mime will scheme to take the Ring for himself, finally achieving his long coveted desire for "top dog" status.

Divinatory Meaning

This card underscores the maxim, "There's no free lunch." It pays to be on your guard with healthy skepticism just now toward an invitation, offer, or gift, as someone's apparent generosity may not be in your own best interests. Scrutinize and research any offers you receive as thoroughly as possible. Trust your gut instinct—especially if it sounds a warning. Remember, timely escape from danger can also be counted as good fortune!

Reversed: You are in an unhappy situation. While you must bide your time for now, don't give in to despair. The circumstance will turn around in time, so maintain a positive frame of mind and trust to the future. A gift or offer is given in good faith.

10 of Nibelungs

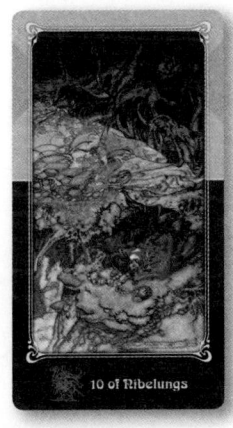

(Rhinegold, Siegfried)

generations of *The Ring Cycle* pass, this legendary glittering treasure loses none of its appeal or its hold on the imagination. Siegfried alone, of all who obtain possession of this wealth, is immune to its corrupting influence.

Divinatory Meaning

This is a card of material success. An inheritance or other monies may be coming your way. A prize is won! You achieve a financial/material/career goal. Perhaps an investment of time or money pays dividends.

In addition to income, however, the gold here also represents personal achievement and well-being. You reap well-earned recognition and respect from others.

The Card: The Golden Treasure Trove

Here is Alberich's fabulous treasure trove accumulated by use of the Ring of Power he fashioned from the stolen Rhinegold. By forswearing all love forever, he was able to steal the precious solar metal from its guardian Rhinemaidens, and fashion it into the fateful Ring. As the

Reversed: There is a setback or delay where money or income is concerned. And keep in mind that "all that glitters is not gold."

2.
Ring Cycle Tarot Spreads

The 3 Norns Spread

The Norns are the daughters of Erda and Wotan. Urdr the Past, Verhandi the Present, and Skuld the Future spin, weave, and cut the thread of human and world destiny. They represent The Fates in the Northern Tradition (Icelandic, Old Norse, and Old Germanic) from which Wagner drew inspiration for his *Ring Cycle*.

Easily and frequently used, this basic three-card spread can yield a surprising amount of information and insight.

2.
Ring Cycle Tarot Spreads

The NIBELUNG Smithing Spread

The Nibelung dwarves are the Artisan/Craftsmen of *The Ring Cycle*. This spread is based on the process of metalsmithing, of which the Nibelungs are experts, being earth elementals and thus masters of minerals and mining.

1 CARD
ORE—Something Important or Valuable Now Hidden

2 CARD
MINERAL VEIN—A Clue From the Past

3 CARD
MINING—Means of Retrieval

4 CARD
REFINING—Opportunity

5 CARD
ANVIL—Support

6 CARD
HAMMER—Impacting External Force

7 CARD
CHASING—Needed Effort

8 CARD
POLISHING—Your Hopes

9 CARD
ARTIFACT—Outcome

2.
Ring Cycle Tarot Spreads

Ring Magical Implements Spread

Central to *The Ring Cycle* are magical tools, objects, and implements. Here are fourteen of them in an interpretive spread, which can be shortened as desired.

1 CARD
RING of FIRE—Your Challenge

2 CARD
SWORD NOTHUNG—Your Strength

3 CARD
RING of POWER—What Compels You to Move Forward

4 CARD
VALHALLA—Your Immediate Goal

5 CARD
GRANE—What Gives You Speed and Energy

6 CARD
WORLD ASH TREE—What Gives You Staying Power

7 CARD
WOOD BIRD—What Your Intuition Tells You

8 CARD
TARNHELM—Your Creative Imagination at Work

9 CARD
WOTAN'S SPEAR—What Grounds or Disciplines You

10 CARD
DRAGON'S BLOOD—Deep Insight

11 CARD
FREIA'S GOLDEN APPLES—A Source of Protection

12 CARD
HAGEN'S POTION—What You've Forgotten

13 CARD
THOR'S HAMMER—What You Need To Summon

14 CARD
SIEGFRIED'S HORN—Your Call To Action

PART III
APPENDICES

In 1901, a decade before his *Ring* art, Rackham illustrated this scene from the Edda (also one of Wagner's sources) for a children's magazine.

Quick Reference Card Meanings

Trumps/Major Arcana

0 FOOL—Siegfried Reforges Nothung

Peak experience: being "in the zone."
Fearlessness.
Innovation and imagination.
Edgework.
"Beginner's mind."

Reversed: Lack of grounding; recklessness and dangerous naiveté. Delusion.

I MAGUS—Loge Summons Ring of Fire

Dynamic will and vital energy.
Creative brilliance.
Clarifying light.
Good timing.

Reversed: Cunning and trickery—a con artist or deceiver at work; poor timing.

II HIGH PRIESTESS—Erda Prophesies

Intuition, deep insight, and discernment.
The Divine Feminine; the powers of the Earth.
Prophetic dreams.
Recalling ancient memories, information, and past lives.

Reversed: Blockage of Inner Light or Voice; seeing surfaces instead of discerning substance and meaning.

III EMPRESS—Fricka Seeks Wotan

Forcefully speaking your own mind.
Adherence to tradition and established institutions.
A mature married woman; the sacrament of marriage.

Reversed: Confrontation; irrationally rigid thinking; separation or divorce.

Quick Reference Card Meanings

IV EMPEROR—Wotan Revises His Orders

Structure and order; responsibility and solidity.
Authority and law take precedence over personal feelings.
Pragmatic leadership.
Paradigm of patriarchal power.

Reversed: Follow the heart not the head; be guided by the spirit, rather than the letter of the law; sincere feeling overrides the rules.

V HIEROPHANT—Valkyrie Brunnhilde

An Initiator who upholds Timeless Truth and Old Wisdom.
Discovering the higher purpose in life experience.
Encountering The Mysteries.

Reversed: Refusing to heed sage advice; feeling betrayed; being unprepared for a test, trial, or initiation.

VI LOVERS—Sieglinde and Siegfried

The Path with a Heart.
Open to the inspiration of connection.
Union and relationship.
Knowledge of polarities through Eros.

Reversed: A broken connection to either your own heart's desire, your higher self and true purpose, or to another person.

VII CHARIOT—Grane

Speed, journey, and the Spirit of Adventure.
Alignment of physical, emotional, and mental bodies, resulting in controlled balance and endurance.
Forward movement. Victory.

Reversed: Spinning your wheels in place; delay; lack of control and loss of balance.

VIII STRENGTH—Sword Nothung

Summoning unusual energy and power.
Defending one's interests with flair, verve, and originality.
Overcoming old conditioning and adaptation.

Reversed: Failure of will and loss of nerve; motivation is needed!

IX HERMIT—Wanderer Wotan

The search for truth.
Observation and information gathering that may involve a battle of wits.
Being in hiding, in disguise, or wearing camouflage.
Solitary pursuits and protracted thought.

Reversed: Show up and participate as your authentic self. Drop the protection of a false persona.

X WHEEL of FORTUNE—The Norns

Energies are in dynamic motion: Process and Momentum.
Destiny and Fate in the field of time.
Luck: Time to take a risk.

Reversed: Standstill or a reversal of fortune.

XI JUSTICE—Wotan's Spear

A decision or negotiated settlement based on law and reason.
Allow restraint and accountability to temper personal will.

Reversed: A miscarriage of justice needs to be addressed.

Quick Reference Card Meanings

XII HANGED WOMAN—Brunnhilde Bound

Dilemma and crisis point precipitating something new.
Breaking old patterns; adopting a different perspective.
Delving deeply into the core gold of the self.
Positive surrender for a greater good.

Reversed: Reluctance to let go of the past; maintaining outworn habits, actions, or ideas. Are you failing to reorient when needed?

XIII DEATH—Valkyries

A sudden and unexpected numinous event or encounter.
Release and Detachment—a great "letting go."
Experiencing Precognition/Second Sight.

Reversed: Denying the inevitable; holding on too tight.

XIV ART—Tarnhelm

A magical occurrence, perhaps shape-shifting, invisibility, swift transport.
Dynamic escape.
Aid from elementals (gnomes, fairies, undines, sylphs, salamanders).
New, unsuspected, or latent abilities.

Reversed: Magic, beauty, and power are lacking! A call for more imagination!

XV DEVIL—Ring of Power

Fateful entanglements: addiction and dependency.
Temptation, obsession, bondage.
Secret vices, especially regarding power or control.
Acting contrary to your own deep convictions.

Reversed: Escape from any of the above.

XVI TOWER—Valhalla

Unstable foundation.
False security masking a fatal flaw.
Dramatic change that may, however, ultimately prove liberating.
A life-changing, sudden realization.

Reversed: A stable situation; well-founded optimism.

XVII STAR—Freia

The Golden Apples of Renewal are at work.
Beauty and Radiance.
Inspiration, Aspiration, Hope.
Possible work with children or youth.

Reversed: Ennui—lack of energy, enthusiasm, or optimism.

XVIII MOON—Rhinemaidens

Listen to your body and to Nature.
Trust your instincts and intuition in a situation: heed a warning!
Imaginative artistic insights.

Reversed: Shifting tides; changeability and fluctuation; unreliability in relationships. A potent but fleeting "high"; intoxication, fantasy, illusion, even delusion. Loss of direction.

XIX SUN—Natural Rhinegold

Illumination from the depths.
"Everything is here and it is good."
Joy, delight, triumph, and truth.
Recovery from illness or misfortune.

Reversed: A blockage of light and energy or delay of all of the above.

Quick Reference Card Meanings

XX AEON—World Ash Tree

Time is Up! The only constant is change.
Completion of a cycle in the Field of Time with a consequent Qualitative and Energetic Shift.
Greater Powers are at work behind appearances.

Reversed: The end is in sight, but there is still time to re-evaluate a plan or change course.

XXI WORLD—*The Ring Cycle*

A Dynamic and Magnetic totality establishes a new equilibrium.
Renewed ideals power a higher turn of the spiral.
World Service and spiritual growth.
Transpersonality.

Reversed: Worlds may collide; additional work is needed to finish a plan or project. Keep on keeping on!

SUIT of GODS—FIRE (Wands):
Spirit & Action

ACE of GODS—Heights of Valhalla

The sky's the limit!
Take advantage of heightened energy and perspective.
High ideals and aspirations have support now.

Reversed: Fluctuating inspiration; a broader perspective is needed.

2 of GODS—Hugin and Mugin

Think and remember!
Do important exploration and reconnaissance.
Detach and delegate needed tasks.

Reversed: You may lack pertinent information; do not give away your power.

3 of GODS—Brunnhilde in The Wild

Take a "time out" to think through a dilemma.
You may be questioning authority.
Act for the Greatest Good in the long run as you see it.

Reversed: Don't waffle; blindly obeying misguided orders will not serve you; don't keep silent or hold back: your voice needs to be heard!

4 of GODS—Cavorting Rhinemaidens

Guarding and Care-taking The Light.
Celebrate, Dance to the Music, Let the Good Times Roll!

Reversed: Do not let your guard down; pay attention and keep your focus! Not time to kick back or play.

Quick Reference Card Meanings

5 of GODS—Fading Immortality

A desperate state of affairs.
You endure a pressure situation as time runs out.
Disagreeing factions erupt.

Reversed: A Resolution is found; crisis is averted at the eleventh hour.

6 of GODS—Wotan Exiles Brunnhilde

"Master & Commander" Card—you set the rules and terms being "Top Dog."
Triumph and Victory.

Reversed: Short-lived victory; a decision goes against you; a farewell results in possible heartbreak and sorrow.

7 of GODS—Giants Take Freia Hostage

You are hostage to a situation not of your making—remain calm and patient.
Try raising your efforts to a new level, as others work on your behalf.

Reversed: A solution from "out of the blue" redeems a difficult situation.

8 of GODS—Ride of The Valkyries!

The high energy and vitality card of the deck.
Plans achieve complete alignment resulting in inspired action.
"Flying" with a project or idea.

Reversed: Confusion and misdirection; losing sight of the goal; going in circles.

9 of GODS—Loge Feigns Fear

Playfulness and a light touch reinforce your position.
Acting on a perceptive insight wins the day.

Reversed: Beat a hasty retreat in a confrontation as you are overmatched.

10 Of GODS—The Giants Examine A Ransom

An agreement is finally honored.
Payment is made for a past debt or service.
Expect imminent release from a restricting situation.

Reversed: Being held hostage to an idea, habit, or circumstance; blinded by the obvious; weighed down by material concerns.

PAGE of GODS—Thor

An unexpected opening appears as a new path is revealed.
Clearing after bad weather.
Powerful protection.

Reversed: Storm warnings! Shelter in place until the weather changes.

KNIGHT of GODS—Cunning Loge

You glean pertinent new information.
Careful listening followed by quick thinking saves a situation.
Engage actively in the present moment, rather than fantasizing about the future.

Reversed: Beware of opportunism; do not reveal information that can be misused.

Quick Reference Card Meanings

QUEEN of GODS—Brunnhilde's Fire Initiation

An all or nothing card: Trial by Fire.
Full commitment is the best course of action in this situation.
Peak experience, Apotheosis, Initiation.
Move beyond the need for approval, and act instead on your true core beliefs.
Serve your vision of the future.

Reversed: Do not leap impulsively; restraint and reassessment are advised; you are not yet adequately prepared for a test or trial.

KING of GODS—Wotan Observes from Safety

Wait and watch, observing carefully from the sidelines.
Bide your time, working at a safe distance for the best result.
Strategically employ what you know.

Reversed: Do not attempt to lead at this juncture; instead, delegate power to capable supporters.

SUIT OF WALSUNGS—WATER (Cups):
Heart & Feeling

ACE of WALSUNGS—A Forest Glade

Setting out on an adventure or quest.
Entering unknown, arduous but fascinating territory.
If challenges are met and tests successfully completed, great potential is realized.

Reversed: Playing it too safe by staying only with what is familiar. Lacking nerve, you are unprepared for an adventure just now.

2 of WALSUNGS—Sieglinde & Siegmund

A high indicator card for romantic love.
There is union and mutual commitment.
Achieving an inner balance of animus and anima within the psyche.

Reversed: Romantic tests and challenges ahead; unrequited love or a short-lived affair. Projecting your own feelings onto another.

3 of WALSUNGS—Sieglinde, Siegmund, Hunding

A short-lived reprieve, as there are enemies in your camp.
A power struggle percolates beneath the social surface.
You begin piecing together a puzzling situation.

Reversed: Find safety in numbers and spend time with friends.

4 of WALSUNGS—Brunnhilde & Grane

Take a reinvigorating "time out" in Nature; commune with animals.
Choose the high road and enjoy the view.
Well-being and good luck are yours for the moment.

Reversed: An unexpected turn of events; or a change of orders.

Quick Reference Card Meanings

5 of WALSUNGS—Sieglinde in the Wilderness

Dig deep and keep moving!
Self reliance and perseverance are necessary now.
You encounter struggles and difficulties, but aid is ahead.

Reversed: Reprieve from a seemingly hopeless situation.

6 of WALSUNGS—Orphan Siegfried Observes Wolves

Nostalgia for happy times past or those yet to be.
Longing for different circumstances, especially related to family.
You remain in the dark with unanswered questions.

Reversed: Close observation leads you to new conclusions; you recognize your true home.

7 of WALSUNGS—Siegfried Challenges Dragon Fafner

Take bold action now!
Be willing to fight for yourself and your beliefs.
You are equal to a difficult or dangerous encounter at this time.
Move forward unafraid.

Reversed: Do not be lured into a fight you cannot win; the odds are against you; retreat and rethink your plan.

8 of WALSUNGS—Waltraute Implores Brunnhilde

A confrontation of differing values.
Stand your ground and hold to your own beliefs in the face of opposition.
Refuse a tempting offer by simply going your own way.
Search for the Higher Good in a complex situation.

Reversed: Selling yourself short, acting from expediency, or buckling under external social pressure.

9 of WALSUNGS—Siegfried Discovers Brunnhilde

At the top of your game, you discover something of great value.
You achieve Mastery, as all good things come to you now.
Possible meeting with a kindred spirit or soulmate.

Reversed: You have climbed to the summit but what you seek is not there; you are following a false trail, so retrace your steps.

10 of WALSUNGS—The Love Call

High Noon in Overachievers' Heaven.
A meeting of the minds ensues.
You experience peak emotional satisfaction and high self-esteem.
A celebration; possibly an engagement or marriage.

Reversed: Delayed gratification; expectations remain unfulfilled.

PAGE of WALSUNGS—Young Siegfried

Seek self-reflection and contemplation in Nature.
You find a clue that solves a puzzle and reveals an answer.

Reversed: Slow down and think more carefully; actively seek new information; a solution to a family problem remains elusive for now.

KNIGHT of WALSUNGS—Rhinemaidens Entreat Siegfried

Listen carefully to an important warning from the Feminine.
Trust any signs, portents, or synchronicities you observe, especially near water.
Kindness, compassion, and patience for others will greatly aid your cause now.
Honor a request.

Reversed: Temper your skepticism, egotism, arrogance, and overconfidence as they will be your undoing.

Quick Reference Card Meanings

QUEEN of WALSUNGS—Sieglinde

Act on your strong intuition and compelling feeling.
Dare to discover the truth!

Reversed: You are backpedaling, perhaps fearing the truth. Are you refusing to honor your deepest feelings in a matter?

KING of WALSUNGS—Siegmund Claims Nothung

An unexpected gift confers confidence, élan, and optimism.
For a limited time, you have unusual strength and power.
In romance, loyalty between partners increases.

Reversed: Strike while the iron is hot and take immediate action; in romance, however, expect complication or delay.

SUIT OF GIBICHUNGS—AIR (Swords):
Mental Plane

ACE of GIBICHUNGS—Winter Storm

Nothing is as it appears. Proceed carefully.
You are enveloped in a swirling external atmosphere of unspoken, unacknowledged, turbulent thoughts.
Gathering opposing forces threaten your plans, yet there is light at the end of the tunnel.

Reversed: A storm passes over you; the air clears, as all involved welcome an opportunity to deal openly and "come clean."

2 of GIBICHUNGS—Brunnhilde and Hagen Plot

Don't jump to conclusions or act in haste.
You may not have all the facts regarding a situation.
Balance is needed; strive to be fair.
Any participation in plots and counter-plots will backfire.
Acting from revenge or other low emotions will bring serious regret.

Reversed: Misunderstandings abound; carefully and openly state your position.

3 of GIBICHUNGS—The Fatal Hunt

Watch your back!
You may be the target of betrayal, jealousy, envy, or revenge.
A situation of pain, deep suffering, or loss.

Reversed: You experience a dramatic reprieve and narrow escape as a plot is uncovered; give thanks and gratitude!

4 of GIBICHUNGS—Rhinemaidens Bait Alberich

In a battle of wills, don't underestimate an opponent.
Unthinking actions and failure to read a situation correctly could provoke explosive change—tread carefully.
An apparent equilibrium proves unstable.

Reversed: An uneasy balance of contrary energies and opposing forces is precariously maintained.

Quick Reference Card Meanings

5 of GIBICHUNGS—Alberich on the Offensive

A *winner take all* paradigm.
Winning and losing in the cyclic battle between light and dark. Denial of both personal and collective wounding thoughts leads to tragedy.

Reversed: "Going for the gold" by making a bold, decisive, and radical move; but be sure to share any prize or resource to achieve a win/win solution.

6 of GIBICHUNGS—Rhinemaidens Report Rhinegold Theft

You suffer a painful loss due to a lapse of attention or judgment. Be certain a call for justice and restitution reaches a truly impartial authority.

Reversed: When making or hearing an urgent appeal, don't let your thinking be submerged in the high emotion of a fleeting moment.

7 of GIBICHUNGS—Fafner Attacks Fasolt for the Ring of Power

A surprising outbreak of anger erupts, fueled by unspoken resentments.
A permanent rift or serious argument between partners or siblings ensues.

Reversed: Defuse anger through conciliation on your part; this is the time to be generous in both spirit and with material goods!

8 of GIBICHUNGS—Revengeful Alberich

Is your pain body full of negative thoughts blocking your true potential? Move on to a positive agenda now by releasing perceived past injustices.

Reversed: It is time to do the necessary inner work to free your mind of a hurtful past.

9 of GIBICHUNGS—Obsessing Alberich

A need to dominate others will only prove isolating and destructive. Harsh judgments or crippling perfectionism inflict cruelty on yourself or others.
Examine a mental obsession that may be ruling your life, preventing you from enjoying happiness in the present

Reversed: Do you feel manipulated? Or are you manipulating others? Escape the gloom and lighten up! Change the scenery.

10 of GIBICHUNGS—Rhinemaidens Triumphant

A card of justice served and fair restitution.
Restoration and recovery after a long ordeal.
You achieve a surprising improbable success against long odds.

Reversed: Futility and hitting bottom—your plans fail entirely. You need to begin again by going back to square one; observe extreme caution near water just now.

PAGE of GIBICHUNGS—Innocent Siegfried

An offer may not be in your best interests; keep your wits about you.
Inexperience can cause serious miscalculation or mistakes.
It is time to acquire more knowledge or training relevant to a pursuit.

Reversed: You have forgotten something of crucial importance. Is someone using you?

KNIGHT of GIBICHUNGS—Dynamic Alberich

Unusual mental energy and powerful help from an outside source is now available.
Utilize these quickly and effectively, as their influence may prove short-lived.

Reversed: Learn from past mistakes by readjusting your intentions accordingly. Examine your own motives—do they serve your highest good?

Quick Reference Card Meanings

QUEEN of GIBICHUNGS—Gutrune

Step out of the shadows and into the light of recognition! Declare your dreams and desires more openly by going public.

Reversed: Someone seemingly friendly may have a hidden agenda; thoroughly examine who stands to gain before making any agreement.

KING of GIBICHUNGS—Hagen, The Power Behind the Throne

Apply the power of concentrated thought to a specific goal. Work out a solution to a difficult situation by thinking it through. Carefully plan a course of action step by step. This card could indicate that a worthy adversary is in your field.

Reversed: Your thinking is misdirected; clear your mind of selfish goals and unworthy, shortsighted plots: negativity will only boomerang. Apply more light!

SUIT OF NIBELUNGS—EARTH/DISKS/COINS/PENTACLES
ALL THINGS MATERIAL

ACE of NIBELUNGS—Earth Chasm

There is new opportunity for worldly success.
Something of great value is hidden in a secret place—what is it?
What is needed to uncover it?

Reversed: Something valuable or desired is currently veiled or obstructed.

3 of NIBELUNGS—Fearful Craftsman Mime

Master your fear and claim your power.
Take pride in your creative gifts.
Don't sell yourself short or allow others to misappropriate your work.

Reversed: Another's power-tripping undermines your efforts; you need to address your lack of self worth.

2 of NIBELUNGS—Alberich Enslaves Mime

A situation of unequal power, forced work, or enslavement.
Submission to an external or internal taskmaster.
Payment of a material obligation comes due.

Reversed: Freedom from a previous restriction or commitment; reinstatement of position.

4 of NIBELUNGS—Alberich Steals the Rhinegold!

A breach in security results in a theft.
There is a concurrent loss of power.
Something you have been relying on suddenly fails.

Reversed: You need to be swifter and dive deeper off the mark; or you escape a situation by making a run for it.

Quick Reference Card Meanings

5 of NIBELUNGS—Mime Forages In the Snow

You may feel you are out in the cold, but you are on the brink of a helpful discovery.
Generosity toward others now will be well rewarded.
You may soon assume a caretaking responsibility.

Reversed: You are acting from a sense of duty rather than love; resentment builds from shouldering responsibilities.

6 of NIBELUNGS—Fafner Guards His Treasure

Play a waiting game.
Don't act until you are fully prepared to meet a challenge.
Careful calculation is necessary to move past an obstacle.

Reversed: Are you being overprotective of someone or something? Break old habits by trying new things; share your ideas, expertise, and resources instead of hoarding them.

7 of NIBELUNGS—Alberich and Mime Argue Over Spoils

There is contention over ownership, money, or intellectual property.
Threat of a lawsuit is possible.
Don't be intimidated: firmly stake your claim in the face of opposition.

Reversed: Just rewards are apportioned; you win a dispute or judgment.

8 of NIBELUNGS—Mime in Wotan's Shadow

Ask the right questions for pertinent information.
Remember, you never know to whom you are speaking; someone unlikely may have the answer you seek.
Do not act impulsively, overconfidently, or arrogantly.

Reversed: Admitting you don't have all the answers leads to productive dialogue; you learn what is really important to know through apparent serendipity.

9 of NIBELUNGS—No Free Lunch

Scrutinize any offers you receive and remain on your guard.
Heed your gut instinct regarding a seemingly generous person.
Remember: there's no free lunch.

Reversed: Compromise is necessary in the short run, providing a temporary stalemate; bide your time and a situation will turn around.

10 of NIBELUNGS—The Nibelung Treasure Trove

Material success: the prize is won!
A generous gift, inheritance, or promotion is in your future.
An investment pays dividends.

Reversed: Where money or income is concerned, there is disappointment or delay. "All that glitters is not gold."

PAGE of NIBELUNGS—Siegfried at Mime's Forge

The Will To Form artifacts, projects, or enterprises.
Success results from inspiration and élan, rather than from studied skill.
Unexpected grace benefits an endeavor.
Securing a birthright.

Reversed: Frustrated, incomplete attempts; a plan or project does not come together; reformulate your process.

KNIGHT of NIBELUNGS—Blacksmith Mime

Intense application and focus.
Inspired, creative, and magical work.
Mastery, skill, and craftsmanship.

Reversed: Do you have the needed skill set or mindset for a creative challenge? Learn from past mistakes and readjust your approach.

Quick Reference Card Meanings

QUEEN of NIBELUNGS—Grimhilde
A Woman Bought with Gold

Are you selling out for status, money, privilege, or position?
The expedient easy choice may not serve your long-term interests.
You experience regret over a past decision.

Reversed: Examine the hidden costs of an offer; act from integrity.

KING of NIBELUNGS—Enslaving Alberich

Assuming "King of the Hill" status.
You may have both wealth and power now, but be on your guard against abusing them.
A false sense of superiority will lead to your undoing.

Reversed: Your leadership ability is currently blocked; more self-discipline is needed; a possible material loss.

2.
Biography of ARTHUR RACKHAM
(1867-1939) Ring Illustrator

Arthur Rackham's 64 *Ring* illustrations, from which I've devised this Tarot, were inspired by his attendance at the 1909 Bayreuth Festival, where he and his wife saw the four music-dramas directed by Wagner's son, Siegfried. The musical performance stirred Rackham deeply, inspiring in him a potent re-imagining of the Nordic and Old Germainic worlds. The "Wagner Craze" was then going strong with attendance that same summer including such luminaries as Virginia Woolf, Alban Berg, and Thomas Mann.

Rackham spent the next two years on his *Ring* illustrations, a high point of his art. Already a professionally well-established and well-known children's illustrator of fairies, pixies, and goblins, he found the greater scope of this adult epic an exciting new challenge. Rackham depicted the Wagnerian gods, elementals, Rhinemaidens, and Valkyries on a sublime level. These illustrations "embody his comprehension of the Nibelung realm as an involuntary devic kingdom" (biographer Derek Hudson) with its unforgettable dwarves, caves, crevasses, and trees. Rackham's *Ring* illustrations were originally published in two volumes: *Das Rhinegold and Die Valkyrie* in 1910, and *Siegfried and Gotterdammerung* in 1911. His original paintings were exhibited in Paris in 1912, where they won the prestigious Societe Nationale de Beaux Arts Gold Medal.

Rackham's "feel" for the *Ring* mythology was also rooted in Germany as his longstanding favorite holiday destination, and he had attended Bayreuth twice before this 1909 *Ring* epiphany: he saw the 1897 *Ring* production, but "returned deceived," experiencing the sets as pedantic and mood destroying. Yet he traveled to another Bayreuth *Ring* in 1899, probably in response to the enthusiasm of George Bernard Shaw, a frequent guest at the Rackham home musicals and parties. Self-described as "an old pal of Rackham's," Shaw, who published his brilliant, witty and still very current *The Perfect Wagnerite* in 1898, undoubtedly stimulated Rackham's continuing interest in this material.

Born into the London middle class, Arthur Rackham was one of twelve children. While a family rumor circulated that a Rackham ancestor had been a pirate, his father was a thoroughly respectable Admiralty civil servant. Art, however, was chronicled in the family tree: his maternal great uncle had been a lithographer and drawing master. Rackham excelled at art—his first love and true ambition—but also at mathematics, and he prudently began adult life as an insurance company statistician. But after graduating from the Lambeth College of Art, he apprenticed as an illustrator for newsweeklies and children's magazines. By his mid-twenties, Rackham was off and running as a successful book illustrator.

In his early work, Rackham shares a special secret with his audience—by revealing the ever-active living elemental world of plant, fairy, and nature spirits who weave and sustain Earth's vegetable and mineral kingdoms. Rackham was able to perceive and describe

2.
Biography of ARTHUR RACKHAM
(1867-1939) Ring Illustrator

this beautiful, super-sensible, etheric world, once a common ancient birthright according to Rudolf Steiner, but now invisible to most humans. By imbedding this hidden energetic realm in children's book illustrations, Rackham unveiled it for generations of youth to see and experience for themselves. Rackham, although perhaps unconsciously, nonetheless inserted knowledge of a secret spirit world into the cultural imagination of his predominantly scientific rationalist Edwardian mainstream. Fred Gettings, author of *Arthur Rackham*, maintains that:

> It is in the realm of the invisible world of spirit that Rackham's true contribution has been the most powerful. Rackham drew and constructed that world through which we peer into soul life.

Chronicles of Narnia author C. S. Lewis describes his own youthful "mystical joy" on seeing a volume of Rackham's *Ring* illustrations displayed in a bookstore window:

> First you must realize that at that time, Asgard and the Valkyries seemed to me incomparably more important than anything else in my experience. His pictures, which seemed to me then to be the very music made visible plunged me…into deep delight. I have seldom coveted anything as I coveted that book…I knew I could never rest until it was mine. I got it in the end…

Art critic and Rackham biographer Fred Gettings surmises this was how Rackham's *Ring* illustrations (along with Wagner's music) fulfilled a "soul-need" of that time, and how wonderfully "creativity rays out into the Future"—even if unknown to its originator.

It wasn't until after I completed this *Ring* deck that, as previously noted in my Preface and Introduction, I realized these illustrations were executed at the same time as Pamela Coleman Smith's for the Rider-Waite deck! I find this quite an interesting synchronicity, considering Rackham evinced neither interest nor any knowledge of Tarot whatsoever!

At the time, however, and in spite of critical success, the published *Ring* illustrations did not meet sales expectations. Released just several years before the outbreak of WWI, they hit the book market as tensions with Germany were already rising. Once war actually broke out in 1914, all things Germanic were naturally anathema in Great Britain. After the war, life in Europe and England dramatically changed: a pre-war artistic climate that had been enthusiastically expansive and innovative was now both financially and psychologically restrained as the Edwardian era luxury book market had collapsed.

Rackham returned to his formerly proven sales status as a well-known children's book illustrator, never deviating professionally from it again.

Both Rackham and Wagner shared a particular artistic sensitivity and vision of a fantastic Nordic natural world full of vital powers and awe-inspiring forces not easily controlled.

But as personalities, the two could not have been more different: where Rackham (Virgo) was steady, careful, and abstemious, Wagner (Leo) was turbulent and extravagant. By all accounts, Rackham was cheerful, methodical, and business-like—all things Wagner was not! Rackham's personal life was as outwardly regular and uneventful as Wagner's was dramatic and volcanic.

As a child, I had the good fortune to see books Rackham had illustrated, such as *Mother Goose, Grimm's Fairy Tales* and *Wind in the Willows*, which made a great and lasting impression on me. Later, as a young artist, I acquired the Dover reprint of Rackham's *Ring* illustrations, that directly inspired this Tarot. I have manipulated some of these images by collaging and adding hand painting to craft them into individual Tarot cards.

One goal I have for *The Ring Cycle Tarot* is to help bring Arthur Rackham's wonderful art—inspired by Wagner's compelling transcendent music—in the form of this interactive divinatory deck, to the appreciation of a new and wider audience.

3.
The Ring's Great Themes

The Ring Cycle, the epic cycle of four Music Dramas by Richard Wagner (1813-1883), first performed together as a whole in 1876 at the Festspielhaus, Bayreuth, Germany, is arguably the greatest single artistic work of the nineteenth century. Composer Edvard Greig compared The Ring to the work of Michelangelo. Performance time runs approximately sixteen hours in length. Wagner conceived the first of the four music dramas, The Ring of the Nibelung, as an evening prologue, followed by one and one-half days of performances of The Valkyrie, Siegfried and Twilight of the Gods.

The Ring's profoundly serious cosmic conception with its immense scale in time and space and its epic spirit creates a lofty and complex musical and dramatic architecture exhibiting many interpenetrating layers of thematic and symbolic meaning. Interpretations have abounded and keep expanding. "Endlessly renewable" is prolific Ring commentator John Culsack's description.

Adding to the Ring's greatness is the sheer volume of secondary works of art, musical, and literary criticism, and philosophical and political discussion it has engendered. Certainly Arthur Rackham's sixty-four illustrations, from which this Tarot is devised, could head the list. The Ring also inspired the great nineteenth century French lyric poet Baudelaire, who enthused that hearing Wagner was "an ecstasy inspiring in him the ambition to make music with words alone."

In the following essay, I select and discuss some of The Ring's themes that I think are among the most important, currently relevant, and not generally discussed in the existing literature.

Time and Eternity
Erda's Prophecy of a Transitioning World Age

Wagner's *Ring Cycle* lends itself readily to a divinatory model by virtue of the dire prophecy deeply imbedded in its core plot. At the end of the *Cycle's* Prelude, *The Rhinegold*, Erda, the timeless Earth Oracle (the German word for earth is "erde"), whose life-span is by far greater than that of the gods, issues her dark prophecy of doom: "All that is, ends. A dark day dawns for the gods…"

This prophecy impels the action of the next three music dramas by inciting Wotan's deep need to comprehend it, resulting partly in the Valkyries, his nine daughters by Erda. Wotan follows this with a further genetic strategy of conceiving the Walsung Siegfried to regain control of The Ring and avert the downfall of the gods (at least by the Nibelungs). Erda's Prophecy is second only to the forging of the Ring of Power as a device that drives the plot of the entire epic.

Wagner found his template for Earth Oracle Erda in the medieval Icelandic (via Scandinavia) Poetic *Edda*, which begins with The Prophecy of the Seeress Voluspa, who, in addition to many other things, foretells the downfall of the gods and a cataclysmic end to their world:

* "The fates I fathom   * yet farther I see
* "Of the mighty gods   * the engulfing doom."

The Seeress or female Diviner was an important figure in Old Germanic and Norse traditions since ancient times. Caesar chronicled how the tribes of Gaul (France and Germany) refused to go to war until their women elders concluded a divination describing the time to be propitious.

Wagner rescued the Feminine Oracle from the "dustbin of history," by restoring her—via Erda—to a position of pivotal importance in his epic. Consequently, *The Ring Cycle* is imbued with the mystical powers of the supernatural. (Thus, a *Ring Tarot* as a divinatory tool seems to me entirely consistent with Wagner's own ideas.)

But what is implied in Erda's prophecy of the end of the gods and their world?

In this particular myth I believe Wagner creatively responded to energies he was personally perceiving and experiencing. His own world was "shifting gears" as a result of many factors, including the eclipse of Christianity as the most important artistic and cultural impulse, along with the radical alteration of both society and the natural landscape due to the impact of the Industrial Revolution. Wagner was also an active participant in the political revolutions that swept through Europe in 1849; he only escaped arrest in Germany by fleeing to neutral Switzerland. So change, and the downfall of regimes, were things he experienced personally.

3.
The Ring's Great Themes

But beyond that, I think Wagner unconsciously apprehended an even greater cyclic shift just over his horizon: and that is the change of Astrological Age from Pisces to Aquarius due to the Precession of the Equinoxes. What Wagner describes—and predicts through Erda—is an entire World Age Transition, to which he alludes in terms of the planet's successive ruling races who shift from gods to humans. In this we can glimpse something of the esoteric doctrine of the Root Races, each of which is described as bringing into Earth evolution new and unique qualities of consciousness.

Precession is the imaginary orbital circle the earth pole traces against the backdrop of the constellations as it wobbles on its axis. Every 2,160 years, the sun rises at Spring Equinox in a different zodiacal constellation (sign) from the perspective of Earth. Each successive zodiacal sign brings in an influx of new energies, qualities, and forms: what is old dies out (gracefully or not), and a different cultural paradigm emerges.

One way history records this phenomenon is in the changing "alpha" animal symbols that are depicted in world historic religious pantheons, architecture, art, and decorative motifs (lions for the Age of Leo, cows and bulls for the Age of Taurus, rams for the Age of Aries, fish for the Age of Pisces).

While I'm not suggesting Wagner was intentionally veiling "The Age of Aquarius" in *The Ring Cycle*, I am suggesting that like all great artists he sensed and intuited a changing cosmic cycle long before any others saw it—before he himself consciously knew it. It's why he was drawn to this particular material. This kind of intuitive foresight—clairvoyance even—is not uncommon among our very greatest artists. And Wagner was a futurist who mined the ancients for evidence of guiding eternal truths that were ignored by nineteenth century scientific rationalism and materialism. Erda, in an important sense, voiced Wagner's own precognition.

Erda births time through her three Norn daughters: Past, Present, and Future. Precession—a longtime cycle by human standards—is a World Age predetermined by an astronomical cycle, a function of time.

Transitional "edges" between changing Ages can last nearly three centuries and are usually difficult cultural periods. Distinctly differing energies war with one another, as the world simultaneously experiences competing "birth pangs" and "death throes." Famous astrologer Dane Rudhyar describes the feeling as being caught between shifting gears in a car.

Such a world in transition is what Wagner depicts in *The Ring Cycle*, and it is one with which we can surely identify, as we rapidly move forward in our new millennium and the incoming Aquarian Age. Erda is the wild untamed feminine and her prophecy is revolutionary, alarming, and utterly disruptive to the comfortable world of the gods. And while she galvanizes Wotan into transforming his consciousness, it is Erda's daughter, the Valkyrie Brunnhilde, who finally evolves into the heroic agent fulfilling Erda's prophecy of world transition.

World Initiation

Finally, we come to the most esoteric idea implied and described in *The Ring*: that our planet Earth, itself a living entity (Gaia-Erda), is experiencing a spiritual initiation of its own—taking every human cell along for the ride!

Earth is a non-sacred planet currently undergoing the process of becoming a sacred one, according to the Ageless Wisdom. (Planets already having achieved sacred status include Mercury, Venus, Jupiter, Saturn, Neptune and Uranus). To this end, our conscious Earth Entity is described as experiencing the Fourth Cosmic Initiation, necessarily entailing upheaval and challenge. The result is described as the transfer of energy from the third Planetary Solar Plexus Chakra of will and power, (embodied by Wotan), to the fourth Planetary Heart Chakra, (represented by Brunnhilde).

"Aggression and greed must be transmuted in the furnace of pain and fiery agony, and will be changed into the power of sacrifice, of inclusive surrender, of clear vision, and the principle of sharing." (Rays and Initiations, p. 520)

A further part of this Planetary Initiation is the dissolution of old group structures (the reign of the gods in *The Ring*), with its now timeworn ideas and old, lifeless, crystallized forms. Wagner envisioned a new Europe and a renewed Germany, in particular, all his life.

It's not surprising then to find that this is exactly what transpires in *The Ring*. Brunnhilde, by acting from the impetus of the inspired heart and alone among all the inhabitants of her world, transcends the will to power and domination, by willingly surrendering the Ring of Power to its rightful guardians.

Initiation insures that things will never be the same. Wagner does not describe any of the end results of world initiation in *The Ring*. Yet implicit in his final music is hope and the redemptive possibility of the next higher turn of the world spiral. The music epic ends with inspired possibilities for our planet.

In witnessing *The Ring Cycle*, we experience a huge, rising, changing planetary tide on both the deeply personal and collective levels—a tide, announced by Erda, that sweeps in tremendous change not only for these mythic northern gods, but for ourselves as well. Our uneasy, perhaps subconscious, recognition of the greater planetary cyclic and precessional oscillations, I believe, accounts for why Wagner's *Ring Cycle* continues to imaginatively fascinate and grip us from a resonant depth of which we are barely aware: the work's dramatic and sonic evocation of over-arching astronomical transitions, which we not only witness as an audience, but in which we ourselves are integrally and wholly—if unconsciously—experientially enmeshed is but another example of why *The Ring* endures as a profound and timeless masterpiece.

3.
The Ring's Great Themes

Cosmic Fire

FIRE is undoubtedly the central and most important image/motif in *The Ring Cycle*, present in all four music dramas in some form and culminating in the fiery apocalyptic conflagration of *Twilight of the Gods*. Wagner's use of fire as a descriptive metaphor for the motive creative force, (the forge), for protection, imprisonment, and initiation (The Ring of Fire), for destruction and transmutation (Siegfried's Funeral Pyre) and finally for purification and regeneration of the entire world, is a scintillating, ever-mutating symbol linking all four music dramas of *The Ring Cycle* together.

In *The Rhinegold,* fire is personified as the wily trickster elemental god Loge and is present in the fire of the Nibelung forge in which the fateful Ring of Power is formed. In *The Valkyrie,* fire is the soothing warmth of the hearth that lures Siegmund into Hunding's hut, as well as the punishing Ring of Fire Wotan summons to imprison Brunnhilde; we hear it flickering in the all-time favorite "Magic Fire Music."

In *Siegfried,* we encounter fire again at Mime's forge, where the orphan Siegfried remakes his father's sword Nothung. Wotan as Wanderer is backlit by this same fire, as he later searches for the Ring's whereabouts and wagers with Mime. Siegfried, overcoming both dragon Fafner's fiery breath and the protecting Ring of Fire, subsequently awakens Brunnhilde.

But the most memorable and terrible fire is saved for the end of *Twilight* in the unforgettable immolation of Brunnhilde and the purifying conflagration that consumes and obliterates the entire world of the gods.

Wagner's use of fire employs the metaphysical-esoteric idea, both ancient and contemporary, of Cosmic Fire. According to the Ageless Wisdom, the Western Hermetic Mysteries, and Divine Alchemy, Cosmic Fire is the super-sensible substrata of all substance in our universe, manifesting in differing forms on all planes of existence. Cosmic Fire burns in the infinitesimally small atomic nuclei, in infinitely huge star giants and galaxies, along with everything else in between, both sentient and non-sentient. It is the living divine spark that powers the cosmic entelechy. Even the Judeo-Christian Bible describes God as an "all-consuming fire."

According to the doctrine of Cosmic Fire, there are four types of fire. I identify the physical fire of friction metaphorically as Loge, the astral fire of passion and desire in the two pairs of lovers Siegmund-Sieglinde and Siegfried-Brunnhilde, the solar fire of ideas in Wotan's will, and the electric fire of spirit in Brunnhilde's self-sacrifice.

Again, similar to the idea of precession, I am not asserting that Wagner was consciously encoding the doctrine of Cosmic Fire in *The Ring*. Nonetheless, we can identify the presence of all these underlying fires within it. Wagner either borrowed or re-imagined the Greek pre-Socratic concept of Heraclitus that all things originate in and return to fire through continual flux as a philosophic underpinning for *The Ring*. This idea was transmitted in the ceremonies of the Rosicrucians, the Masons, and through the illuminated manuscripts and practice of alchemy—all of which fed the nineteenth century primarily male intelligentsia in the manner of an underground spring. Wagner, with a reputed interest in Rosicrucianism, would have certainly encountered the idea and imagery of a subtle, all-pervading, life giving, transforming, transmuting, and transfiguring divine Fire.

Flying under the official academic and institutional radar, the concept of a scientifically indiscernible, yet primal Fire as an energetically animating and mutable principle percolating within all substance, was an important, if unacknowledged, influence on the era's artistic and cultural thought. It seems plausible Wagner adopted the alchemical principle, Igni, Natura Renovatur Integra (all nature is restored by fire) as a fundamental idea with which he vivified his *Ring Cycle*.

3.
The Ring's Great Themes

Gold Lust and Greed

The entire *Ring Cycle* has been interpreted by several commentators as the shadow of the Industrial Revolution. Alberich the loveless dwarf initiates and oversees the desacralization and enslavement of the Earth's elemental kingdom in his incessant mining and hoarding of its mineral wealth, for which gold is the symbol. It is this fundamental betrayal of the feminine principle by the patriarchy in the external rape of a disrespected Nature and in the consequent imbalance it perpetuates, that hastens the dramatic eclipse of the gods.

The struggle for gold/mineral wealth among nations and the power it confers has been the cause of many a world conflagration—the twentieth century's two world wars at the end of the Age of Pisces are an example. The recent war in Iraq for "Liquid Gold" is another.

While it is little known today, Wagner held the lifelong political ideal of a society freed from the curse of gold (Mann). Interestingly, Wagner started writing *The Ring* libretto in 1848—the same year the Gold Rush began in California. Given Wagner's belief that gold lust was the primal curse of mankind (rather than knowledge as the Bible has it), this synchronicity to me is telling; and I believe *The Ring* is, in part, meant as a critique of it.

Wagner embodied the nineteenth century conceit that art, replacing a corrupt and distorted religion, could redeem society. In his art Wagner saw "a means of salvation for a corrupted society… he dreamed of an aesthetic consecration that should cleanse society of the greed of gold" (Mann).

Alberich's renunciation of all love forever is what allows him to steal the pristine gold, and it is this renunciation and this theft that initially sets off Wagner's mythic epic.

This was the great curse of mankind as Wagner saw it—the lust for gold, which is really the deep need, born of insecurity, pain, and separation, for establishing power over others. In *The Perfect Wagnerite*, Shaw observes that this "Plutonic power is so strongly set up (as a result of the Industrial Revolution), the higher human impulses are suppressed as rebellious…"

Wagner is perhaps the first to apprehend the New Age idea of "Ancient Future."

Inspired by the myth and symbolism of a distant past, he consciously fashioned a work incorporating its ideals that was dedicated "…to the creation of a new world and a new order of freedom and creativity" (Burnett James). In *The Ring*, Wagner issues the warning that the quest for purely material wealth and world domination, with its requisite denial of love, will prove fatal to all civilizations. Once unleashed, Gold Lust cannot be contained, and it will inevitably wreck worlds.

Racial Conflict and the Struggle for World Power

The Middle-Earth of Wagner's *Ring Cycle* (like that of Tolkien's *Lord of the Rings*) is populated by a number of different races who jockey for position, power, and control in their respective worlds. While generally maintaining an uneasy, peaceful coexistence, they are sometimes in open conflict.

Four of these races include the gods, the demi-god Walsungs, the Gibichung humans, and the Nibelung dwarves, who I have used for my four Tarot suits. Other *Ring* species include the giants and the water elemental Rhinemaidens. While not necessarily distinct races, the Valkyries and the Norns, all daughters of Earth Oracle Erda, also inhabit unique genetic niches.

The gods are clearly the ruling class of *The Ring*. In *The Rhinegold* King Wotan has entered into a secret construction contract with two giant (working class) brothers, and has agreed to give them the Goddess of Beauty and Immortality, Freia, as payment for building Valhalla.

But Wotan, arrogant in his sense of privilege and entitlement, never really intends to honor his pledge. Wotan believes that by virtue of his superior intelligence and social status, he is free to manipulate the "slow learner" giants at will. The giants want only the payment that had been previously agreed upon. But when they ask for their fair wages, Wotan backpedals and stalls.

George B. Shaw identifies this as a management-labor class conflict, in which the workers have fulfilled their part of the agreement, but the bosses are out of integrity and do not want to pay up.

A second racial conflict is between the gods and the Nibelung dwarves. The dwarves are much brighter than the giants and know better than to trust the self-serving gods. Alberich, who by virtue of the Ring of Power, has become the Nibelung ruling tyrant, now has the means to challenge the gods for world supremacy. Motivated primarily by jealousy and envy, but also by past grievances, including the humiliation of being treated as inferior, Alberich is bent on displacing and punishing the ruling gods "to get even." Injustice and revenge continue to be underlying causes contributing to political revolution and war in our own world.

In *The Valkyrie,* demi–god Siegfried relates his repeated problems with humans to Sieglinde. He is always in conflict with them over core moral values and is consequently ostracized from their settlements. The inference is that the demi-gods have a higher sense of both personal freedom and justice than the barbarian humans, whose sole standard is brute physical force. Consequently, the two cannot easily coexist. In this we might extrapolate our current world political conflicts that result from the collision of divergent historical experiences and differing cultural/ social assumptions.

3.
The Ring's Great Themes

In *Siegfried* the conflicts are more parental (between Siegfried and Mime) and generational (between Siegfried and Wotan) than they are overtly racial.

However, in *Twilight*, Nibelung Alberich continues his quest for world domination, if only to prove that a (lowly) dwarf is capable of establishing superiority over everyone else. Alberich's strategy is one of obsessive relentless cunning and a forswearing of any and all love—forever. He's the negative example of "the pain body" attempting to achieve personal and political power at the expense of every other being. He's a racial ego completely out of control (the Germany of WWII immediately springs to mind).

The Ring's view of racial tensions and conflicts seems to be one of sober realism—that differing biologies necessarily result in differing temperaments, outlooks, assumptions, and values. Intrinsic to the model of a single racial elite ruling the world will be the inevitable unending chafing and jostling of the disempowered to get to the top. Implied in *The Ring Cycle*, (and totally missed or ignored by Hitler and the Nazi Party) is that a different and inclusive political model is necessary for social justice and lasting racial peace.

Love, Sacrifice, and Redemption

We come with great relief to these truly healing powers of *The Ring Cycle*, of which Brunnhilde is the shining exemplar. I believe Wagner's true message is ultimately the positive one that the highest human achievement is to evolve consciously, and that this can only result from cultivating a love of the entire world.

Love

The Valkyrie leader exhibits nothing but love for all with whom she interacts (except her irascible stepmother Fricka, who is loved by no one we ever see).

She loves her father and King, Wotan; she loves her sister Valkyries; she loves her magical horse Grane; she loves her half brother and sister, Siegmund and Sieglinde; she loves Siegfried.

* All Brunnhilde does, she does for love.

* Is it her undoing or her great salvation?

It all depends on how we interpret her final immolation. My view is that Brunnhilde's deep love is what propels her beyond herself, into Initiation as a world server, allowing her to finally act as the Evolutionary Agent of World Destiny. In spite of her revengeful and uncharacteristic complicity in Siegfried's murder, her capacity for selfless love is what finally distinguishes her from and elevates her above all the other *Ring* characters.

While Siegmund loves Sieglinde and Siegfried loves Brunnhilde (and to some extent possibly Gutrune), the scope of both their romantic loves prove limited and they die too young to develop it beyond the personal.

And while Wotan attempts to love his offspring—and he does seem capable of love—he proves too conflicted in his emotional core to maintain the strength of any love he may actually have. He is distracted from love, first by his rulership of the world and then by his alienated renunciation of the very world he rules!

Sacrifice

We generally think of sacrifice as having to give up something we really desire to keep and that it consequently demands pain, suffering, and loss. But sacrifice can actually indicate greater synchronization with a higher energy. We let go of something smaller and of lesser worth, because we know that this will ultimately allow us to gain something

3.
The Ring's Great Themes

greater and more valuable in the future. Sacrifice, in this view, is really then not so much a *giving up* as it is a *trading up*. In spiritual sacrifice, we strive to release that light that was previously hidden and unseen, but which we are now able to perceive.

Brunnhilde, while forced to sacrifice her Valkyrie leadership and her status as a god, gains first, human love (which Wagner clearly considers more valuable) and then her ultimate destiny as a World Change Master. The spiritual Law of Sacrifice employs a dynamic use of will, a fixed determination, and a focused heart to be effective. I would say Brunnhilde's ultimate act of self-sacrifice combines all of these.

But there are other kinds of sacrifices in *The Ring* as well. There is Wotan's ritual sacrifice of his demi-god magical twins Sieglinde and Siegmund and the pivotal sacrifice of "the world hero" Siegfried. The sacrifice of the twins is exacted by the gods to maintain civil temporal law. Siegfried, in contrast, is sacrificed on the cross of world imperfection by the dark powers of involution.

Siegfried must be eliminated if Alberich is ever to regain the Ring of Power and proceed with his plan for a world takeover. So, the murder of Siegfried is also a political assassination; thus Siegfried is symbolic of all noble and good leaders who in their attempt to bring more light into the world are eliminated by the opposing powers of night.

In this sacrifice of the impetuous, spontaneous, and instinctual Siegfried, we can also see the sacrifice of our own youthful optimism

and exuberance to the constricting harsh economic and social order of the substantially more sober, literal, and material adult world. Jung interpreted the sacrifice of Siegfried as symbolic of the necessity of humans to censor a part of our deep inner natures in exchange for the benefit of being able to live together in collective societies (something Siegfried was unable to achieve).

Redemption

Trump XXI WORLD—THE RING CYCLE, pictures a Brunnhilde transcendent—one who has redeemed Alberich's Curse, the Rhinegold, and finally her entire world all at the same time.

In addition, she also redeems herself from the profound personality grief and remorse of Siegfried's death. While her personal redemption is both admirable and necessary, it is the higher transpersonal redemption that *The Ring Cycle* primarily addresses.

Redemption counters those forces that hold back the evolution of consciousness on all planes—individual, planetary, cosmic. So it may also be described as fundamentally a *release of light*. Part of our human destiny, according to esoterics, is to help "release the prisoners of the planet." The idea is that our mandate in becoming co-creators on Earth includes, in part, our working with the mineral, vegetable, and animal Kingdoms of Nature to help them develop their unique innate powers in achieving their own consequent greater consciousness.

Both art and science can be a means of doing so (though not the only means), especially when motivated by a love for the world as a divine vehicle.

At the same time, we must work to free our individual consciousness from imprisonment by our own personality illusions and glamours. We are only able to redeem substance, as well as ourselves, when we work toward the spiritual integration and harmony of everything. So we might posit a Unified Field Theory with the redemptive power of Love as the ultimate Building and Binding Force.

And in *The Ring Cycle* Brunnhilde embodies this redemption by furthering the planetary evolution of consciousness and releasing it from the confining strictures of the compromised gods who cannot manage their own world.

4.
WAGNER'S RING MUSIC
More Than You Ever Wanted To Know

As previously stated, *Ring Cycle*, the epic cycle of four Music Dramas by Richard Wagner (1813-1883), first performed together as a whole in 1876 at the Festspielhaus, Bayreuth, Germany, is arguably the greatest single artistic work of the nineteenth century.

The Ring as music retains its popularity and relevance today because of its radical originality and sheer orchestral beauty, displaying profound psychological insight, metaphysical profundity, and raw dramatic power.

In his *Ring,* Wagner concocted a heady magical potion mixing equal parts world revolution, mythological depths, and human psychology at its cutting edge. These were all scored to some of the greatest and most original Western orchestral music ever written. *The Ring*, according to Thomas Mann, is a spell wrought by a deeply serious and completely ravishing magician.

The Ring, like all ultimate truth, is a paradox. The story and characters are tragic and dark. All who embody brightness or Light meet early, untimely ends, thwarted and betrayed by envy, greed for power and wealth, or misunderstanding. Yet the music itself is transformative, luminous, highly evocative of other shimmering world possibilities, remaining still (and perhaps forever?) unfulfilled. In contrast to the forcefully deep shadow cast by plot, characters, and fate, the opalescent music opening onto sublime uncharted vistas is what we ultimately take away with us and remember. It is Wagner's music of transcendent promise—not the fiery conflagration destroying the gods— that draws us back again and again to *The Ring*.

Perhaps it is just this philosophic tension between the tragic/pessimistic plot line and the optimistic music of promise that fuels, at least in part, the artistic greatness of this cycle. "It's difficult to deny that the close of *The Ring* may have been intended as a musical statement... that subverts, after all, the sense of inevitable end," writes John Culshaw in his *Twilight of the Gods* DVD notes.

It seems that Wagner's intuitive musical optimism, like a powerful shaft of sunlight, broke through the dense forest gloom of his philosophic pessimism, in spite of himself.

Virginia Woolf described Wagner's music in her 1909 essay "Impressions at Bayreuth" as making "...a very deep and perhaps indescribable impression…the music has reached a place not yet visited by sound."

Wagner the composer opened a new musical vein described by Burnett James in *Wagner and The Romantic Disaster* as "supreme subjectivity." In contrast to Beethoven, who expresses the (ultimately successful) personal struggle of self-affirmation, self-determination, and freedom, Wagner submerges the individual in an irrational mystical experience of a refined and intoxicating mingling of all the senses, in which the self can be lost, completely enveloped within sound, color, and fragrance. As history has proved, this suspension of the rational faculty has its unique dangers: one person's "sublime vast metaphysical vista" is another's "narcotic fog" in which an ungrounded susceptible self may become disastrously absorbed and disoriented—with terrible consequences, as history has demonstrated, especially if applied on a national scale.

Truly Wagner's *Ring* music can be a seductive opiate that often proves blissfully addictive. It is necessary "to give oneself over" entirely to the *The Ring Cycle*, to experience its full effect, and this does suggest the metaphor of ingesting a mind-altering drug—explaining, perhaps, why such a highly refined voluptuary as Baudelaire was so wholeheartedly enthusiastic about Wagner's music.

There is no doubt that *The Ring,* like all great art, demands our interest, time, effort, sustained attention, and reflective thought. And like all great art, it also pays tremendous dividends if we can find recognition in it and maintain the necessary stamina for it.

Could it just be possible, as Nietzsche thought, that art is the highest human task and the truly metaphysical pinnacle of life? Could the Maya, who investigated and understood the nature of time as profoundly as any known world culture ever has, actually be correct in their declaration that, "Time Is Art"?

4.
Ring Music
More Than You Ever Wanted To Know

The Ring Libretto and Its Sources

Among Wagner's radical innovations as an operatic composer was that he wrote all of his own librettos—he never used anyone else's text for his music. Traditionally, composers chose writers, poets, and librettists to set the dramatic text to which they wrote their musical accompaniment. Wagner, however, wrote both his own text and music. Given his innovative use of the "Orchestra as Text"—at times reminiscent of the ancient dramatic Greek Chorus that comments from a detached perspective on the stage action—writing both words and music was a necessity for the original, seamless music-drama "art of the future" that Wagner envisioned.

Wagner's sources for *The Ring* included the *Norse/Viking/Icelandic Prose Edda*, *The Poetic Edda*, *The Saga of the Volsungs*, and the *Old Germanic Nibelungenlied*. These are ninth to thirteenth century texts that recorded traditional oral epics many centuries older.

Wagner is often faulted for altering these traditional story lines and characterizations. But he did so, not for the sake of change itself or out of sheer egotism, but because he had his own specific creative, artistic, and imaginative ends in mind that were currently relevant to him and his nineteenth century audience.

One of these aims, in accordance with the nation building of Europe at that time, was to craft a new National German Art.

Wagner was making a pointed statement in presenting his King of the gods, Wotan, not as the all-powerful Shaman, Bard, and wise political leader of the old epics, but instead as a beleaguered pragmatic monarch scrambling to maintain his regime from collapse by internal contradiction and external insurrection. I believe Wagner purposely adopts this contrasting depiction to illumine the moral and spiritual failures of the modern world, in order to confront and heal them.

He was also highlighting the belief of the European intelligentsia, that "the gods were dead" and could not be relied upon for help of any kind. Humans now have to rely on themselves to solve their problems.

The Music-Drama Leitmotif

The *Ring* music is not "tuneful" in the manner of operas before it: it contains few traditionally singable melodies, distinct arias, ensembles or expected finales. "There is not a single bar of classical music in *The Ring*," George Bernard Shaw asserts in *The Perfect Wagnerite*.

"It is too much to ask that it (the E flat bassoon opening sustained note of *Rhinegold*) be called music. It was not: it was an acoustic idea" writes Thomas Mann in the same vein. And these are *The Ring* enthusiasts! What is going on? This describes Wagner, the innovative composer, at his most radical.

He employs the orchestra not just in a secondary role as accompaniment to his singers, but instead as a distinct and separate "speaking voice" that tells its own highly subtle and psychologically complex tale, full of reflections, reminiscences and foreshadowing. "In Wagner, the orchestra always tells the truth" asserts Maestro James Conlon—even as the characters themselves dissemble due to egotism, malice, or plain ignorance.

The vocal line can be entirely different from and often seemingly unsupported by the orchestra. Singers and orchestra must weave in and out of each other, contributing equally to creating the complex tapestry of human voice and symphonic sound that is the music drama. Wagner's brilliant innovation and use of "Literature as Music" and "Music as Literature" remains unequalled. Similar to the precision of ancient Mayan mortarless fitted stonework, Burnett James describes "the impossibility of slipping a knife-blade between the joints and joins of Wagner's text and music."

Wagner achieved this music-drama meld through the inspired use of the leitmotif—a descriptive musical phrase associated with a particular character, emotion, or object. Wagner's orchestral leitmotifs herald the appearance of off-stage characters, describe their hidden emotions and inner thoughts, remind us of their past history, and hint at the coming action. They also describe certain natural and even supernatural forces. Ernest Newman in Volume II of *The Wagner Operas* identifies 198 of these *Ring* identifying musical phrases! Beyond obvious leitmotifs for central characters and objects, such as

4.
RING MUSIC
More Than You Ever Wanted To Know

the Rhinegold, Valhalla, the Giants, and Magic Fire, there are those demarcated for intangibles including Renunciation (of love), the Curse, Annihilation, Magic Deceit, Rapture of Love and Redemption (by love).

Certain passages in Schopenhauer's *World as Will and Representation*, published in two editions prior to Wagner's beginning *The Ring*, read like a detailed prescription for Wagner's music-drama leitmotifs. Schopenhauer discusses how ideally in opera the orchestra " has a wholly independent separate…and abstract existence by itself …which follows its own rules," irrespective of what the singers/actors may be doing on stage. "The words are…for the music a foreign extra of secondary value, as the effect of the tones is incomparably more powerful, more infallible, and more rapid than that of words." Clearly Wagner took all this to heart in devising the method of leitmotif composition for his serious musical dramas.

The less well-disposed critics of Wagner charge that when all is said and done, he cannot really be called a composer; "that all" he does is string together a limited vocabulary of his leitmotifs, albeit in inventive and creative ways. And there is some small grain of truth in this. But if that were the whole of the music, *The Ring* would no longer be heard in continually newly inspired, often purely symphonic, performances and recordings.

It was through the genius of his imaginative, innovative, interpenetrating and texturing of the leitmotifs, that Wagner shaped the symphony into a new medium of an articulately layered psychology descriptive of complex thoughts and involved emotions. Together, Wagner's leitmotifs raise a vast, intricate, awe-inspiring musical architecture before us that is much greater by far than the mere sum of its parts.

Color Music

Another of Wagner's important innovations as a major classical composer was evoking the sound of colors from the symphony orchestra and within his audience's experience. Color chromaticism is a term used with respect to both music and color. In music it refers to discrete tone changes, as the chromatic scale is comprised of half rather than full tones; in reference to color, the term designates use of a wide range of differing hues.

In *The Ring*, Wagner creates diaphanous florescences of orchestral "color vapors" to establish mood and create both a natural and spiritual atmosphere. While not explicitly descriptive, they are highly suggestive—evaporous, fleeting, and intensely personal.

Musical color is not found as a major component or as an end in itself in the work of European composers previous to Wagner, such as Bach, Mozart, and Beethoven, all of whom relied more on melody, harmony, and counterpoint to achieve their artistic ends. Wagner, by evoking the subjective apprehension of color, brings in a new and different musical experience.

This evocation of color in Wagner's music is often experienced as an exploration and description of non-material metaphysical planes. Wagner unseals these realms and vistas, previously closed to the ear, through orchestral color—which is partly what Virginia Woolf means by citing Wagner's work as a new place not previously described by sound.

Rudolf Steiner asserts that color has its origins in the "surging flowing soul-life," and that the life of the spiritual world is the reality that stands behind color.

In experiencing color forces evoked through sound, we begin to touch and penetrate into the domain of our personal and collective soul world. Although it is rarely so expressed, this experience of the soul realm evoked through "the color of sound" with its variation of lights and shadows, I believe, accounts for much of the enthusiasm Wagner's music generates in his listeners.

4.
RING MUSIC
More Than You Ever Wanted To Know

Unending Melos

One afternoon while showing my Tarot in progress to a friend, she expressed her keen displeasure with Wagner's music declaring in utter exasperation that, "The music doesn't have an end!" I laughed, responding that this was exactly Wagner's point!

The Ring as uber music continually flows, constantly changes, forming new and different configurations, and as pure energy, is always conserved within a closed system similar to a universe. But for my friend, as with many people who listen for a single clearly defined musical climax (ala Beethoven) this "unendingness" prevents them from finding their musical bearings. In Wagner's music there is no great relief at achieving a final aural resolution or goal, because any specific goal, as in life, generally changes into another, proving finally elusive, as it continues ever-evolving. There are resolutions, but they sound continual rather than final.

Music, like time, flows of one piece in *The Ring*. It is not tied up in discrete easily digested musical parcels—it is all of a piece, unwinding and transforming, folding back on itself—but never with exact repetition.

Themes and whole musical keys subtly and incrementally change into one another, similar to the way in which light can change over the course of a day in a natural landscape. This characteristic, known as unending *melos* (melody) seems to drive many people (including my friend) mad, but symphonic conductors appreciate it as yet another of Wagner's radically innovative and lyrically beautiful musical ideas.

And while there are sometimes distinct preludes, *The Ring* music for the most part is a seamless dynamic sound continuum slowly and deliberately unfolding a unique musical atmosphere. Beethoven's music is a good contrast in style here because, while it describes psychological and emotional triumph in the outer objective world, Wagner's music references entirely different mental faculties—those of the subtle and shifting intuition, and the inner subjective worlds, where, because of its relative unfamiliarity to many, they may elicit only incomprehension and aversion.

The Ring music does yield great rewards for those who can adjust to the demands of its innovation. "Wagner's music," writes Thomas Mann, "instructs us in what is really passing behind the falling veils."

In other words, Wagner's colors and unending melos lend sublime musical descriptive form to the ceaseless, invisible energies and incomprehensible powers that build and continually sustain our world.

CODA

Wagner's music is often described—even by his critics—as unsealing and exploring new realms. Unveiled by the probing exploration of his innovative compositions, previously unheard and unsensed metaphysical splendors extend our "bearable edge of knowing." Through this superlatively beautiful and original music, a shaft of timeless light illuminates new and high significances for us. In *The Ring of The Nibelung* with its unique meld of myth, drama, operatic singing, and symphonic music, Wagner the composer of new harmonies expands our ability to perceive previously unrevealed supernal lights. In this *The Ring Cycle* music is truly revolutionary

Artistic beauty, in the words of Goethe, "is a manifestation of secret natural laws that otherwise would have remained hidden forever." *The Ring Cycle* music contains this revelatory signature of the very greatest, highest, and most profound art. Through its high appeal to both our senses and to our immaterial imaginations, *The Ring Cycle* is an artistic vehicle through which we can discover deep new truths about ourselves and our world.

5.
Musical Listening Suggestions

For those who have never heard Wagner's *Ring Cycle* before or those unfamiliar with any of the *Ring* music, following is a list of the most well-known excerpts that can serve as a basic introduction to Wagner's powerful and evocative music. I also include *The Ring Cycle Tarot* cards directly relevant to these musical selections.

There are many performances of these on a wide assortment of "Ring Music/Highlights" CD's:

"Entrance of the Gods into Valhalla"
(The Rhinegold)

Ring Cycle Tarot Cards:
Ace of Gods—Valhalla
Page of Gods—Thor
XVI Tower—Valhalla

"The Ride of the Valkyries"
(The Valkyrie)

(I believe everyone will recognize this music. Francis Ford Coppola used it in his film *Apocalypse Now* and it is a longstanding staple of cartoon scores.)

Ring Cycle Tarot Card:
8 of Gods—Valkyries

"Magic Fire Music"
(The Valkyrie)

Ring Cycle Tarot Cards:
6 of Gods—Wotan
I Magus—Loge
XII Hanged Woman—Brunnhilde

"Nothung!"
(Siegfried)

Ring Cycle Tarot Cards:
King of Walsungs-Siegmund
Knight of Nibelungs—Mime's Forge
Page of Nibelungs—Siegfried
0 The Fool—Siegfried
VIII Strength—Sword Nothung

"Forest Murmurs"
(Siegfried)

Ring Cycle Tarot Card:
Page of Walsungs—Siegfried

(While depicting a younger version of Siegfried, this card captures the reflective mood of the music.)

"Brunnhilde's Salutation to the Sun"
(Siegfried)

Ring Cycle Tarot Card:
10 of Walsungs

"Siegfried's Rhine Journey"
(Twilight of the Gods)

No descriptive Ring Cycle Tarot Card

"Siegfried's Funeral March"
(Twilight of the Gods)

Ring Cycle Tarot Cards:
X Wheel of Fortune—The Norns
XX Aeon—World Ash Tree

I also recommend *The Ring, An Orchestral Adventure*, arranged by Henk de Vlieger on a Chandros CD 5060, as an introduction to this music. De Vlieger pieced together some of the above selections into a seamless one-hour symphonic score.

For those interested in delving into the complete music dramas, a good place to begin for a fundamental understanding of the entire epic is the NY Met 1989 Otto Schenk production available as a DVD set. This is a beautifully designed traditional adaptation conducted by James Levine, which your local library may have.

There are also "post-modern" experimental adaptations of *The Ring*, but because they vary in quality, they can be confusing, even to those familiar with Wagner's epic.

6. BIBLIOGRAPHY

TAROT CARD IMAGES

Rackham, Arthur. *Rackham's Color Illustrations for* Wagner's *"Ring."* New York, NY: Dover Publications, Inc., 1979.

Wagner, Richard. *The Ring of the Nibelung.* Translated by Margaret Armour, with Illustrations by Arthur Rackham. New York, NY: Garden City Publishing Co., Inc., 1939.

TAROT

Arrien, Angeles. *The Tarot Handbook.* London, Eng.: Diamond Books, 1995.

Case, Paul Foster. *Highlights of Tarot.* Los Angeles, CA: Builders of the Adytum, 1989.

Crowley, Aleister. *The Book of Thoth.* York Beach, ME: Samuel Weiser, Inc., 1985.

DuQuette, Lon Milo. *Understanding Aleister Crowley's Thoth Tarot.* York Beach, ME: Samuel Weiser, Inc., 2003.

Fortune, Dion. *The Mystical Qabalah.* York Beach, ME: Samuel Weiser, Inc., 1984.

Giles, Cynthia. *The Tarot: History, Mystery and Lore.* NY: Fireside, 1994.

Greer, Mary. *Women of the Golden Dawn.* Rochester, VT: Park Street Press, 1995.

Jyanti, Amber. *Tarot for Dummies.* NY: Hungry Minds, 2001.

Leo, Dai. *Origins of Tarot.* Berkeley, CA: Frog Books, 2009.

Pollack, Rachel. *A Forest of Souls.* St. Paul, MN: Llewelyn Worldwide, 2002.

Skafte, Dianne. *When Oracles Speak.* Wheaton, IL: Quest Books, Theosophical Publishing House, 2000.

Stewart, R.J. *The Elements of Prophecy.* Dorset, Great Britain: Element Books, 1990.

Wang, Robert. *Qabalisitc Tarot.* York Beach, ME: Samuel Weiser, Inc., 1987.

ARTHUR RACKHAM, *RING* ILLUSTRATOR

Gettings, Fred. *Arthur Rackham.* London: Studio Vista, 1975.

Hamilton, James. *Arthur Rackham. A Biography*. NY: Little, Brown & Co. Arcade Publishing, 1990.

Hudson, Derek. *Arthur Rackham, His Life and Work*. London: William Heinemann LTD, 1960.

Spero, James. *Introduction, Rackham's Color Illustrations for Wagner's Ring*. NY: Dover Pub., Inc, 1979.

RICHARD WAGNER'S *RING CYCLE*

Barenboihm, Daniel and Edward W. Said. *Parallels and Paradoxes, Explorations of Music in Society*. NY: Pantheon Books, 2002.

Bolen, M.D., Jean Shinoda. *the Ring of Power: The Abandoned Child, The Authoritarian Father, and the Disempowered Feminine*. San Francisco: Harper Collins, 1993.

Byock, Jesse L. *Introduction & Translation, The Saga of the Vol. sungs, The Norse Epic of Sigurd the Dragon Slayer*. Berkeley, L.A., London: Univ. of CA. Press, 1990.

Chapin, Anna Alice. *Wotan, Siegfried and Brunnhilde*. NY, London: Harper & Bros.,1899.

Cross, Milton. *Stories of The Great Operas*. NY: Washington Square Press, 1967.

Culshaw, John. *Reflections on Wagner's Ring*. NY: Viking Press, 1976.

_____. *Ring Resounding*. NY: Viking Press, 1967.

_____. *Wagner, The Man and His Music*. NY: E.P. Dutton & Metropolitan Opera Guild, 1978.

Davidson, H.R. Ellis. *Gods and Myths of Northern Europe*. Baltimore, MD: Penguin Books, 1971.

Day, David. *Tolkien's Ring*. Illus. by Alan Lee, NY: Freidman/Fairfax Publishers,1994.

Donington, Robert. *Wagner's "Ring" and Its Symbols*. London & Boston: Faber and Faber, 1979.

Graham, F. Lanier. *The Rainbow Book*. Reprint. NY: Vintage Books, 1979.

Hatto, A.H. *The Nibelungenlied*. Baltimore, MD: Penguin Books, 1972.

Heline, Corrine. *Esoteric Music of Richard Wagner*. Santa Monica, CA: New Age Bible & Philosophy Center, 1986.

6. BIBLIOGRAPHY

Hollander, Lee M. *The Poetic Edda.* Introduction and Translation. Austin, TX: Univ. of Texas Press, 1999.

Jacobs, Robert L. *The Master Musicians Series: Wagner.* London, Melbourne, Toronto: J.M. Dent & Sons LTD, 1974.

James, Burnett. *Wagner and Romantic Disaster.* NY: Hippocene Books, 1983

Mann, Thomas. *The Suffering and Greatness of Richard Wagner From Essays of Three Decades.* NY: Knopf, 1947.

Newman, Ernest. *The Wagner Operas, Volume II.* NY: Harper Colophon Books, 1983.

Shaw, George Bernard. *The Perfect Wagnerite, A Commentary on The Ring of the Nibelung.* Chicago & New York: Herbert S. Stone & Co., 1898.

Spencer, Stewart, and Barry Millington. *Wagner's Ring of the Nibelung.* London: Thames & Hudson, 2000.

Spotts, Frederick. *Bayreuth, A History of the Wagner Festival.* New Haven & London: Yale Univ. Press, 1994.

Sturlson, Snorri. *The Prose Edda.* Translated by Young, Jean L., Berkeley, L.A., London: University of CA Press, 1992.

Wagner, Gottfried. *Twilight Of The Wagners.* NY: Picador/Pan, St. Martin's Press, 1999.

White, Michael and Kevin Scott. *Introducing Wagner.* NY: Totem Books, 1995.

Woolf, Virginia. *The Essays of Virginia Woolf, Bayreuth.* NY, San Diego, London: Harcourt, Brace, Jovanovich, 1986.

ESOTERICS

Bailey, Alice A. *A Treatise on Cosmic Fire.* NY: Lucis Publishing Company, 1973.

_____. *The Rays & Initiations.* NY: Lucis Publishing Company, 1970.

_____. *Letters On Occult Meditations.* NY: Lucis Publishing Company, 1970.

Barborka, Geoffrey. *The Divine Plan*. Adyar, India: The Theosophical Publishing House, Vasanta Press, 1998.

Blavatsky, Helena. *The Secret Doctrine: The Synthesis of Science, Religion and Philosophy*. Pasadena, CA: Theosophical Publishing Press, 1988.

De Purucker, G.V. *Hierarchies and the Doctrine of Emanations*. San Diego, CA: Point Loma Publications, 1987.

Pauwels, Louis and Jaques Bergief. *The Morning of the Magicians*. NY: Avon Books, 1973.

Rilke, Rainer Maria. *Duino Elgies and Sonnets to Orpheus*. Translated by A. Poulin Jr. NY: Houghton Mifflin Co., Mariner Books Edition, 2005.

Rudd, Richard. *Gene Keys, Unlocking the Higher Purpose in Your DNA*. London and NY: Watkins Publishing Ltd., 2013.

Steiner, Rudolf. *The Inner Nature of Music and The Experience of Tone*. Hudson, NY: Anthroposophic Press, 1987.

_____. *Colour*. East Sussex, Great Britain: Rudolf Steiner Press, 2005.

Tolle, Eckhart. *A New Earth*. NY: Dutton Penguin Group, 2005.

Tuchman, Maurice, Ed. *The Spiritual in Art: Abstract Painting 1890-1985*. L.A: LA County Museum of Art & Abbeville Press.

7.
EPILOGUE

If by chance or fate you came into possession of the Ring of Power, and were required to perform one act before returning it to the Rhinemaidens, what would you choose?

About the Creator

Allegra Printz is a native of Detroit, Michigan, and attended Monteith College, Wayne State University. A graduate of the Boston Museum School of Fine Arts and a professional artist, her work is in private and public collections throughout sixteen states, Canada, China, and the Netherlands. Her recent book, *Bay Area Landscapes, Pastels, and Oils*, can be viewed online at www.blurb.com

Allegra is a lifelong classical music lover. As a Boston art student, she was a dedicated follower of Professor Roland Nadeau's musicology lectures from Northeastern University. She studied piano and music theory privately in Provincetown, Massachusetts, with Juilliard graduate and composer Richard Busch.

Since the early 1970s, when she enrolled in the BOTA Tarot course, she has acquired many Tarot decks and books, and attended numerous Tarot workshops and symposia with Tarot luminaries Mary Greer, Rachel Pollack, Angeles Arrien, Ed Buryn, and Thalassa. A San Francisco Bay Area Tarot Symposium (SF BATS) Daughter of Divination, she began reading Tarot cards professionally in 2000.

The study of Tarot led Allegra to the discovery of Aura-Soma, a living-color energy system created by Vicki Wall of Great Britain, in which bottles of dual, pure color essences correspond to Tarot cards through sharing Kabbalistic addresses on the Tree of Life Glyph. She became a certified Advanced Level Aura-Soma Practitioner in 2003.

Residing in the San Francisco Bay area, Allegra remains a student of Ancient Egyptian, Indian Vedic, and Tibetan Buddhist texts, Western Hermeticism, the works of Rudolf Steiner, The Ageless Wisdom, and most recently Richard Rudd's *Gene Keys*.